THE GOLDEN AGE OF BRYMBO STEAM

The Golden Age of Brymbo Steam

GEOFF & HUGH CHARLES

'Excellent material and warm, lively narrating.'

ISBN: 0-86381-435-2

Cover design: Smala

First published in 1997 by Gwasg Carreg Gwalch,
12 Iard yr Orsaf, Llanrwst, Conwy, Wales, LL26 0EH.
☎ (01492) 642031

Printed and Published in Wales.

The Authors

GEOFF CHARLES born January 28th 1909. Lived in the Old Vicarage, Brymbo; educated at Brymbo Council School and Grove Park School, Wrexham; won a History Scholarship to King's College London but changed tack to study Journalism. He became President of the Journalism Students' Union and gained a First Class Honours Diploma in Journalism before entering a career in local newspapers (mostly in Wales) as a photo-journalist. The Geoff Charles collection of 120,000 annotated photographic negatives, recording the political, social and cultural life of Wales and the borders, is housed in the National Library of Wales. He has been a member of the Gorsedd since 1984.

HUGH CHARLES born February 13th 1910. Lived in the Old Vicarage, Brymbo; educated at Brymbo Council School, Grove Park, Wrexham and the Technical Institute, Wrexham, before joining the Brymbo Water Company where his father was the Manager. After war service in the navy, on convoy escort duty in the Atlantic and Mediterranean, he spent 18 years working as a water engineer for the Tanganyikan government, rising to be Deputy Manager of the Dar-es-Salaam Water Supply. He was then employed by the Ministry of Overseas Development on projects in Jordan and Nepal before retiring in 1977. He now lives in Spain.

Contents

Introduction

Hugh and I have very happy memories of our childhood. This book is what we like to remember of those early days and does not pretend to be a scholarly history: it is largely what we learned of life in Brymbo amidst the stories of neighbours and the business of growing up.

Railways and trains touched our young lives at every point and were our constant companions; we were reminded of them in all our nightly and daily being. They woke us in the morning, took us to school and brought us home again, gave us a real-life hobby far better than playing with any toys and lulled us to sleep at night. Our friends and neighbours worked the engines and the signal boxes and sometimes, on magical occasions, allowed us to join them at their work. Now, of course, it has all gone. The *Great Western*, the *London & North Western*, the *London & North Eastern*; all of which had steamed into Brymbo, have all departed, and so has the industry they supported.

This book was planned by my brother Hugh and myself as a project for retirement. Without Hugh, this book would never have been completed. Its early progress was threatened by glaucoma and my sudden blindness would have put an end to it had it not been for Hugh. He left his home in Fuengirola to spend much of the autumn with me putting this book together. Without him, these reminders of a vanished way of industrial Welsh life would never have been completed.

We owe an infinite debt to the staff of the Welsh National Library at Aberystwyth; we would like to thank the Broughton & District Local History Group for permission to reproduce the two maps of Brymbo and Mr C.J. Wignall for permission to reproduce the map of railways in the Wrexham area from his book *Complete British Railways Maps and Gazetteer (1830-1981)*.

We would also like to thank Mrs Glenys Gruffydd for her encouragement and support and my son John Charles for reading and correcting the proofs. Even more than is the case for most other books, the production of this volume has really been a team effort.

Geoff Charles,
February 1997

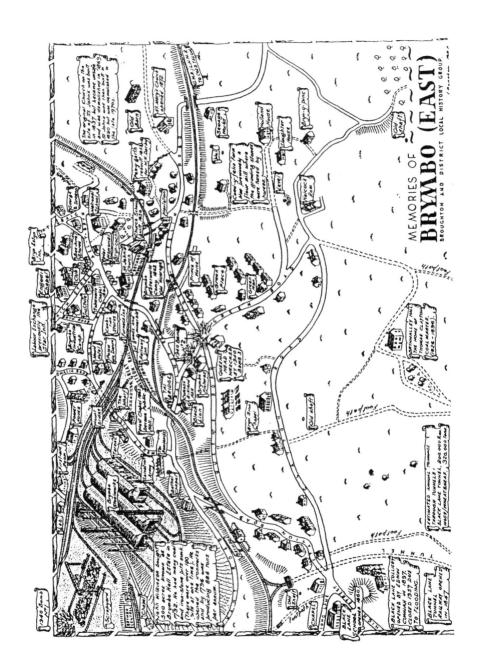

MEMORIES OF
BRYMBO (EAST)
BROUGHTON AND DISTRICT LOCAL HISTORY GROUP

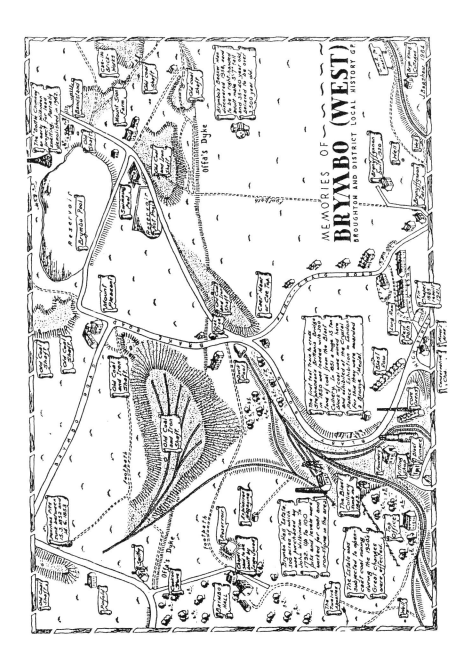

MEMORIES OF
BRYMBO (WEST)
BROUGHTON AND DISTRICT LOCAL HISTORY GP.

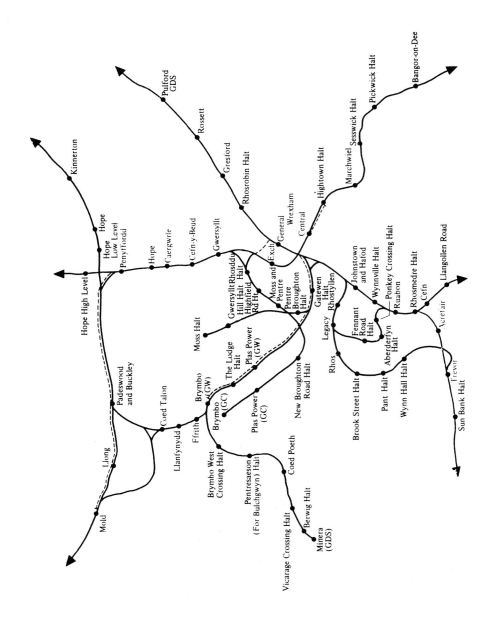

Bangor-on-Dee
Pickwick Halt
Sesswick Halt
Marchwiel
Pulford GDS
Rossett
Gresford
Rhosrobin Halt
Hightown Halt
Kinnerton
Hope
Hope Low Level
Penyffordd
Hope
Caergwrle
Cefn-y-Bedd
Gwersyllt
Wrexham Exch
General
Central
Johnstown and Hafod
Wynnville Halt
Ponkey Crossing Halt
Rhosmedre Halt
Cefn
Llangollen Road
Hope High Level
Moss Halt
Gwersyllt Hill Halt
Rhosddu Halt
Highfield Rd Hlt
Moss and Pentre
Pentre Broughton Halt
Gatewen Halt
Rhostyllen
Fennant Road Halt
Aberderfyn Halt
Acrefair
Trevor
Pant Halt
Wynn Hall Halt
Rhos
Legacy
Brook Street Halt
New Broughton Road Halt
Plas Power (GW)
The Lodge Halt
Plas Power (GC)
Brymbo (GW)
Brymbo (GC)
Ffrith
Brymbo West Crossing Halt
Pentresaeson (For Bwlchgwyn) Halt
Coed Poeth
Berwig Halt
Minera (GDS)
Vicarage Crossing Halt
Coed Talon
Llantynydd
Padeswood and Buckley
Llong
Mold
Sun Bank Halt

10

Chapter 1

Living on the railroad

The story starts in Bryn Awel, Brymbo, where the John Charles family lived. The back gate was only a hedge away from the single track of the *London & North Western Railways'* Mold – Coed Talon – Brymbo railway.

There was a level crossing not a hundred yards from our house. The four big gates were opened and shut by the Patterson family: the father, Sam Patterson was a ganger on the line, and wore 'Yorks'. The house they lived in was railway property; and as well as the gates they had a small ground frame and signal levers to work the signals guarding the crossing. They also operated the points which controlled the access to a small siding. This was a refuge for a coal black Webb tank engine which brought its train to Brymbo Station, stabled there ready to return to Mold later in the day.

My brother and I were then at the age when the magnificence of the big black tank engines paled before Sam Patterson's 'Yorks'. These took our eyes at once; we had so far only known the Brymbo Water Company's men who only wore 'ordinary trousers' and boots. Sam Patterson wore corduroy trousers which were gathered below the knee but above his boots by a thin leather strap buckled tightly. My father explained that this was to keep his trouser bottoms clean when he worked in mud or on oily tracks.

Having settled this important matter – and established our father as he to whom any railway mystery might be referred – Hugh and I then promptly fell in love with steam engines and railways. I am sure we must have sorely tried the patience of my mother and her current 'mother's help', Gwennie, when the glory of steam overcame us. As soon as we could walk we were drawn to the Annie Patterson's gates. As soon as the signal above our house clanked down Annie came out brandishing two very large keys. These she slammed into the locks; a quick turn and we knew the bolts would be withdrawn and the gates would open.

By this time Hugh and I would have chased off to the gates and been pursued there by a panting Gwennie who knew the gates were enough of a barrier. Safely behind them we waited for the engine to come so near that we, safely shielded by the gates felt the heat from the firebox and recoiled from the menace of its great black wheels. We were level with the rails and we watched fascinated as the very rails sagged under the engine's weight and the sleepers stirred in their settings as the wheels rolled on. Annie reappeared holding the keys; a rattling slam in to the gate locks, a quick trot round by Annie and the gates swung clear. But we noticed that the gates were opened so that the one facing the road traffic would be opened first.

My mother had equipped the kitchen in Bryn Awel according to the best standards of the day – a large, solid fireguard rounding the fireplace, a cut-down kitchen chair to make handling small children easier at bath times. I must have been the sort of mischievous child who could not keep still. When I was two, my mother and Gwennie were getting tea ready one evening. My mother had Hugh as a small baby (there were thirteen months between us) and when I asked for something to do to help her, she told me to help Gwennie with the tea. While her back was turned I took the sawn-down chair, put it against the fireguard, and decided to 'help' by taking the boiling kettle off the fire. Luckily it fell off the hob on to the hearth, scalding no-one, but I fell face down on the hot hob. My left cheek and temple were scarred. The only recollection I have of the whole event is the bottle of *Carron Oil* which my mother used on my face. I've never liked big blue bottles since. She did a wonderful repair job: I have been complemented in times of hospital visits on 'the remarkable plastic surgery you must have had'. I have twice been asked by mothers of children with scarred faces if I would tell them what hospital treated my face. I am proud to tell them – no hospital, no Archibald Mcindoe, nothing but a mother's unfailing love and bottles of *Carron Oil*.

Beyond the crossing the rails continued to pass, lower than and to the left of the Old Vicarage, and under Railway Road. The bridge bore a cast iron plate claiming that its iron girders were 'Brymbo made'. Number 16 Railway Road, which we now know as the Old Vicarage, had been my father's family home since the 1860's; Thomas and Mary Charles, my grandparents, had ten children there; two of them, girls, had died, both bearing the same name, a usage of that time.

There was no gas or electricity in Brymbo, but there was plenty of coal. There was an old man called Edward Jones ('Temprance') who had a horse and cart which would be sent to the land sales part of Brynmally colliery, and I think for about seven shillings and sixpence, he'd bring back about half a ton.

In the kitchen we had an old, huge, black-leaded range – I think it was called *The Excelsior*. There was an oven on one side of the fire and it seemed (to me at least) that it was always needing new 'cheeks'. This seemed a painful matter to me and caused my mother and her present maid-of-all work much trouble. It meant a visit to Walter Roberts the Ironmonger in Wrexham: the cheek was an iron casting which diverted the fire's heat towards the oven when needed. Before very long Dad had fitted a *Foresight* range with a 'warm' oven low down. This had rings which could be lifted out so that a pot or kettle or frying pan could be heated. Above it was the oven proper with (my mother was proud) a glass door. But Hugh and I liked the old grate with open bars in front of which we hung a *Dutch Oven*, a light affair with a shallow tin vessel in the bottom to catch the fat that dripped from bacon, kippers or sausage that dangled from the hooks on the top bar of the triangular covering of the oven; a tinplate cover was swivelled from the roof of the oven so it could be used when you wanted to grill the other side of what you once had done. It also of course made toast; that was where Hugh and I made our breakfasts before dashing off to school by the half-past-eight train.

The house had become a Vicarage when Brymbo Welsh Church was built. It had been changed from a traditional Welsh 'long house' by building a square Victorian house at right angles to the old long farm house. Other alterations were made to the original building to make a coach house, stable, and brick floored yard, perhaps for the vicar's coach.

After I became acquainted with Iorwerth Peate, whose pioneering work on folk culture inspired the St Fagan's Folk Museum, I bought his book – *The Welsh House*. Only then did the peculiarities of construction and design of the Old Vicarage make sense.

We moved there from Bryn Awel after my grandmother and grandfather died. My father had been regarded as a confirmed bachelor until a young and pretty Queens' Nurse came to Brymbo to work with the one already established. 'Queens' Nurses' was a charity, inspired, as its title suggests, by Royalty, and was described as a charity to nurse the sick poor in their own homes. They did as much as today's district nurses do: the two nurses had a very neat cottage built for them at the bottom of Pleasant Lane opposite the site of the Railway Crossing.

I am sure that the changes I saw when we moved into the Old Vicarage were of my mother's planning. In front of the kitchen fire were two old wooden settles, their legs buried into the floor. Dad and a workman pulled them bodily out while my mother and her latest 'Gwennie' screamed at an invasion of ants and blackbeetles that followed. Kettles of boiling water stemmed the invasion. A flue ran up to the ceiling and roof of the single storeyed kitchen: this was later plastered over to make it look less agricultural.

To the left of the fire-place in what was the kitchen of the old long house, steps led down to two equal-sized rooms (we would call them basements today) which had been designed to accommodate the farm animals, on the left and their food. On the right a similar division was for more food for humans and animals.

This later became a store room for a paraffin tank which pumped out its contents into an old teapot of my grandmother's which then filled the many oil lamps for the house and offices. It also held a coal fired washing boiler.

Above these two rooms was the long low bunkhouse where, in their early days, my father and his brothers, Thomas Owen, Caradoc, Aubrey and Goronwy had their bedroom and their abode.

It was in this long room that my father decided to put a huge copper cylinder that supplied hot water for the bathroom. The last room of the long house was our sitting room, square and unpretentious. A door opened into the well of the hall from which stairs went up to the three bedrooms. What Dad called 'the vicar's wine cellar' lay to the left of the foot of the stairs, and Dad had wangled into it steps down, a W.C., wash hand basin and full size bath. A short tiled passage led from the bottom of the stairs to the front door, on either side of the passage was a room.

I have read that the long house developed as farms in hilly cold countries. I have seen many examples in Switzerland and Austria where winters can be cold and snowy. Everybody and all the animals lived under one roof, as did much of their winter food. A central division in the farmhouse left room on either side for animals and their feed. Above the family quarters kept warm at night by the animals, just as in old Welsh farms, the 'llofft stabal' over the horses kept the man who looked after them warm.

One thing about the Old Vicarage pleased us all – despite its age and church associations, no one ever thought of any ghostly apparitions until Nain Charles gave my mother, all innocently, a scare after her death. Nain Charles had made a habit of an afternoon stroll down the back land, over the railway crossing to Bryn Awel. Tango, the Old Vicarage Welsh Terrier, also came for his biscuit. He ran on before Nain Charles and usually jumped up on top of the back-garden wall and barked and pranced about until Hugh or I noticed him and went to open the back door. As we did so, we'd shout to my mother *'Mae Nain ar ei ffordd'* – 'Grandma's on her way' or, being good little children of a generation which was seen rather than heard, began to get tea ready for Nain and my mother. As the oldest, my job was to see to the kettle and make the tea; Hugh's was to bring in a tray laid with two cups and saucers, sugar and milk; Margaret, being the youngest, brought the biscuit barrel.

This, of course, we were expected to do without being asked: as soon as we saw or heard Tango we knew Nain would be with us in about the length of time it would take for a pot of tea to brew and so we would immediately set about our tasks.

On one particular afternoon my mother was sitting sewing with her back to the window when we looked up from where we were playing on the floor and, without any comments, began to organise tea. My mother asked us what we were doing; we pointed out of the window and told her that Nain was just arriving. She sat there paralysed, seeing certainty in our faces and actions but knowing what we hadn't yet been told – that the old lady had just died. She couldn't bring herself to turn round and look out of the window; instead she listened horrified as the door creaked open . . . and in came Tango, hoping for a dog biscuit. After Nain Charles died, Tango still came for his dog biscuit every afternoon, and pranced about on the wall asking to be let in. We, full of excitement on seeing Tango thought of Nain Charles and continued to look for her coming. This upset my mother, always a little readily persuaded of other-worldly events, and she began to discuss with Dad whether her two 'innocent' boys might have powers to see things adults had lost. Dad, of course, pooh-poohed it, and that's where it ended.

* * *

To me it was accepted that each time a passenger train went down to Wrexham the whole house stirred. It was a fact of life: it just happened. Accumulations of my father's professional tomes, of years of *Strand Magazines, London Illustrated News* (there was a copy of the report on the Tay Bridge Disaster, when a whole train fell from a cast iron viaduct into the sea). We saw nothing prophetic in this; we accepted it as in some way related to Brymbo since we, too, had a Tai (but not *Tay)* Bridge. Our Tai, of course came from the name of the pub, which in turn gave its name to the Bridge. *Tai* is the plural of *Tŷ*, or house, and gave that name to the tiny hamlet there.

But back to that tall bookcase. When the train passed our house, as I said, the whole house stirred, and the top of the bookcase inclined its head gently towards my bed.

It had a different effect on visitors. I well remember a day when I was confined to bed with a cold. I had a very special visitor that day. She was a red-haired, blue eyed nurse who later became my wife. This visit was in the very early days of our acquaintance and she was very different. As I was warming to the thrill of her unexpected visit, a train went past, I stole a glance at her face and was disturbed to see a look almost of fear: then I saw the bookcase lean slightly back against the wall, and understood.

Chapter 2

Trains, the one transport

It is difficult to realise nowadays that the only transport – to the next town, Wrexham, for example – was the train. But our neighbour in Brymbo, Harry Hughes, a goods guard on the GWR railway kept a pony and trap and it could be hired. The pony was a large factor in my early childhood. Mrs Hughes, who kept the *Railway Inn* across the road from the Old Vicarage, and who sometimes invited Mother, Hugh and me to go for a short ride in their pony and trap, would present herself to us in a completely different guise from her usual pub-landlady's outfit. She usually wore a working apron with what seemed to Hugh and me an enormous pouch of a pocket which represented to us all the mystery of money and commerce. But on the pony and trap, she would be well turned out: large, red cheeked and infinitely capable.

The trap was simple: light with a bench seat for the driver and a passenger or (in our juvenile case) three. There was a strict etiquette. The passengers adjusted their weight by moving forward or to the rear and so making the pony's work easier.

Once during an afternoon's run to Bwlch-gwyn for a fowl (a cold white corpse that Hugh and I regarded with distaste) the pony fell and badly cut its knees. We got out and watched in distress as Mrs Hughes begged my mother to stop the bleeding and comfort the trembling pony. My mother, resourceful as ever, went to a nearby house (it was near the Smelt Cottages) and got water and rags and bound up the knee. Hugh and Mrs Hughes rode back; my mother and I walked home, Mrs Hughes not quite the same confident woman who had driven away from Brymbo. The pony's knee soon healed.

Our new house in Brymbo opened up a new world of railways to Hugh and me. When we finally – at the advanced age of four – were sent to the very new Brymbo Council School, of which I shall have more to say later, the *Great Western Railway* came between us and our education. The bedroom which Hugh and I occupied faced the steelworks and the long curving 'hill' that let the GWR climb from Brymbo Station to Brymbo West Halt and – of much more importance – to the junction just outside our house where the line climbed to Brymbo Steelworks. We soon got to know that the great event was the morning *Hook Norton Express* as my father called it. This brought a train load of iron ore: usually eight 20-ton steel wagons with a brakevan. It was timed to arrive about 8.15 and was usually headed by something new in our railway experience – a 'tender engine'. To those not as aware of railway lore as two small boys with a railway-made father, the usual locomotive used on branch lines at that time was a six-wheel tank engine whose water was carried in tanks usually built on top of the boiler. The 'tender-engine' carried its water in the six-wheeled vehicle which also carried many tons of coal as well as water. This made it, in our eyes, a much more important locomotive.

So, come the morning, two excited small boys would break away from the breakfast table and rush upstairs to see the Hook Norton come up from the Croes Newydd junction on the main GWR Paddington – Birkenhead line and up from GWR Brymbo Station.

For Hugh and myself, when we had progressed to Grove Park School at Wrexham, our morning started when the first passenger train went up to Coed-poeth. Strangely my 1902 copy of the voluminous GWR timetables has 'Up' from Coed-poeth to Wrexham. And it cost my father all of 'One Penny'!

We knew the train would be back at Brymbo West Halt at 8.32 because the North Western Webb tank engine and its three six wheeled carriages ran into Brymbo station at 8.20.

After the passengers had left the train, the engine would 'run-around' the coaches and shunt them into the sidings. If we had lingered over breakfast, Dad, who had heard the North Western engine's three whistle blasts telling the signalman that the train was in the siding and clear of the points, would come to us and say, 'Come along, the North Western has given the 'safe inside', its time you were moving if you want to catch the School train'.

To protect Brymbo, which was a junction and a station of some importance, 'catch points' were installed which would derail a runaway train or vehicle, to send it crashing down the road below!

Trembling with excitement we would see our heroic engine come into sight at the foot of the 'hill', prepared for battle. At first all went well! But if it were a wet morning and what Dad would call a 'greasy rail', the brave charge would end with the engine's wheels slipping impotently. My father, usually breathing down our necks, would say resignedly, 'He's lost

18

her. She's lost her feet. Now he's in trouble!'

The driver could try to coax the engine to find its feet again with liberal sanding of the rails from the engine's sand boxes. As soon as the train stopped the guard would apply his van brakes hard on to hold the train. Guard's vans had special brakes to do this. The driver would let the engine run back a little way until he felt the guard's van brakes hold and then use the considerable 'slack' in the couplings and try to get the engine and wagon train under way. In spite of the sanding the engine would often start slipping again, smoke, steam, cinders cascading up from the chimney, sparks from the spinning driving wheels.

Once the train crew had decided to accept defeat it was all systems go to rescue the train – while two very worried small boys were demanding time checks from their parents. They had to be in school by nine, and school was all of ten minutes away.

To reduce the load on the engine the train had to be halved. The guard would go down the train with a stout brake stick and tighten and pin down all the brakes on the half of the train that was going to be left. In the meantime the engine crew would be taking the chance of a look at the fire and give it a stir up with the 'pricker' to shift any clinker that might be spoiling the fire. Then, the moment two small boys were breathlessly awaiting (worrying about being late for school!): the driver would give the customary blast on the engine whistle, open the cylinder cocks to warm up the cylinder, and drain condensate and with not too much of throttle opening, he'd cautiously try to get the train away. Even half the original train was some load to start on the steep curve. A cough and a groan from the loco, a sudden blast of exhaust from the chimney as she lost her feet for a moment – in the engine cab a hurried dash by the driver for the regulator, a cautious touch on it, and the half train was away safely. And so were two small boys, off down the back lane, past the Plantation, the other big level crossing, past the neat little Nurses Home where mother once reigned, and then up the steep hill to Brymbo Council School.

The large crossing gates were flanked by a low stone wall. Here small boys tired of play could watch Alf Rogers and his mate checking signal wires and platelayers packing ballast under sleepers. We knew that shortly a 'steelworks train' would come down to Brymbo West where the engine would leave the train, cross to the down line passing within feet of our grandstand and using the crossover on the down line would back up to the train waiting for it by Brymbo Middle Box. After the shunter had coupled up, and the guard had given the 'rightaway' the engine and its train came past once again within feet of our wall. The sound of the ponderous wheels and the groaning as they passed us was music to our ears. Sadly all this is in the impossible past: the trains, the crossing gates, Alf Rogers and indeed everything else that made railway entertainment out of so important a task as the railways carried out, has vanished for ever.

From Brymbo West Halt as we waited for the commuters to join our 8.55am train we could see all Brymbo on our left (we always faced the way we were going). Above our heads the rattle of the driver's controls being relayed to the engine footplate signalled our departure. We passed the large water tank on pillars that stood guard above the bottom end of Brymbo West Halt, passed the first World War garden allotment that Alf Rogers had created parallel with the Back Lane. A moment later Alf Roberts house, a glimpse of the Old Vicarage and the Railway Inn. A look at fields between the Mold Line coming in on our left. A rattle over the Mold Line junction and over Brymbo Station Crossings, its gates of course shut to road traffic, then Brymbo Station. This was the original main station; Brymbo West came later. Passengers from the Coed Talon Mold train joined us here; their coaches were put into a siding where the mouth of the old Brake tunnel could still then be seen. A short run down to Lodge Halt, with the bulk of the steelworks on our right and the panorama of Lodge around us. On to Plas Power where the late-night Saturday trains had trouble in getting away after putting passengers down. Through Southsea and a meeting with the Moss Branch, coming in on our left: ahead of us the smoke, steam and smell of Croes Newydd Engine Sheds. When we were going to school enormous stocks of coal, neatly piled and all whitewashed, surrounded the Engine Sheds. After Croes Newydd the branch line swung left on to the main line and into Wrexham Station, passing rows of red brick houses whose gable ends were decorated with painted advertisements for somebody's pills. The advertisements claimed that these pills were 'ALWAYS BOOMING', a statement we perceived as vaguely improper: schoolboy humour, no doubt. As our train drew into the one 'bay platform' allotted to us (the Moss Branch used the other) we had passed what we called 'The Lager Beer Works'. That was our morning ride to school.

Some time after our school train went a second school train left for Wrexham with an 0-4-2 tank engine, usually a Corwen Branch Train. I think this was regarded as a 'girls' special'.

As with other commuters, we got to know our fellow travellers. One very large lady, always immaculately suited, and wafting a most delicious perfume, intrigued us because it was said that as she boarded the train at Brymbo West the carriage tilted. I must confess that although I looked for the phenomenon closely I never in fact saw it. Edward Roberts, Bryn Coch, Brymbo, was often on the train; he was a public man of some eminence and to us, very old. He used to go into the smokers' compartment and I was amazed a man as old as he appeared to be could smoke a fierce and smelly pipe that I, used to my father's *Three Nuns* tobacco, had to keep far away from!

Our trains – the weekday ones – were not unlike in shape and comfort modern inter-city ones. They were not compartmented, but open, and had seats that could be adjusted with swivelling backs so you could 'face the engine' if you preferred. They were steam heated, and – unlike Brymbo houses! – were gas-lit.

There were two coaches of this type and an engine – usually an 060 pannier tank – between them. These engines were fitted with special controls so that the driver could drive the train from either end. The fireman stayed on the footplate and controlled the fire and the boiler. The driver stood in his glass-fronted compartment at either end of the train: in front of him a large regulator control lever hung down to his hand, and brake controls were handy. At his feet was a pedal for clanging a large bell: since the engine was in the middle of the train anyone working on the line might find it approaching him in dangerous silence; so any platelayer on the line would receive clangorous warnings.

Probably the death of Brymbo's Dr Batty, knocked down by a passenger train at Bryn Rhug Crossing, had contributed to the provision of this warning device.

To Hugh and myself, the big deal was Saturday night working. On Saturday night, no more auto trains – pannier tank 0-6-0 engines and what we called 'real train' of compartment carriages. For the 6.55 from Brymbo West Halt to Wrexham, arriving at Wrexham six minutes past seven on a Saturday night, there might be a hundred passengers. The 8.10 from Brymbo got to Wrexham at 8.21; the 8.50 at 9.03. An added attraction to us was that they did not use the bay platform, but arrived on the main Paddington – Chester line platform. Going back from the thronged station you had a choice of ex Wrexham 8.50, Brymbo 9.05, or 7.20, Brymbo 7.45.

Often with well-loaded trucks, there'd be drama on the up trains at Southsea station, when the engine tried to start the heavy train again and the same at Brymbo. Brakes 'leaking on' was Dad's verdict: it meant that train staff had to get under the train to balance brake cylinders with a lot of to-ing and fro-ing and an occasional bit of swearing, when someone hit his hand instead of what was intended. Eventually the engine managed to blast its way upward to showers of sparks from the chimney. Hugh and I felt it a fitting end to an interesting day.

When I first travelled on these coaches as quite a small boy, I noticed in the guards' 'vestibule' as I entered the train a large lever which was arranged to control something big under the floor. Research showed that this controlled large steps tucked away under the coach. My usual fount of railway lore – my father – explained that the railways were conscious of traffic being lost to buses – the GWR pioneered buses in Pwllheli and Llŷn – and sought a means of enabling passengers to flag a train down anywhere on its tracks and board it.

But what about the long – very long – step up to the train, probably from the track side and treacherous ballast? So this was the solution – folding steps that popped up when the guard threw the lever. Many 'halts' were wooden erections and guards were issued with bus-type tickets so that a passenger who had not had a chance to buy a ticket at a formal booking office could pay his or her fare.

This system was adopted on the steam motor trains too, and although in my younger days the conductor could issue your ticket, I never saw the lineside steps used.

Occasionally, we would have on the Brymbo and Moss branches what Hugh and I and Dad knew as 'the Moss Motors'. These were a development of the same idea – a sort of a steam motorbus on rails. The GWR called them Rail Motor Vehicles and made – or had made – the first of them early in 1903. The idea was tried in 1847-49 on the *Bristol & Exeter and Eastern Counties Railways*, but the *Great Western* borrowed one of Dugald Drummond's Steam railcars built for the *Fratton & Havant Services* on the forerunners of the *Southern Railway*. George Jackson Churchward designed similar vehicles for the GWR and soon it became the greatest user of these rail motors and other South Wales railways also built and used them.

The Moss and Coed-poeth branches had these rail motors which were carriages with a vertical boiler built into the front of the coach driving a small steam-engine 04-0 bogie. Both driver and fireman had an enclosed weather proof footplate, but most enginemen preferred an open footplate – at least the ones I knew did.

At Wrexham station, two bay platforms were used by Moss and Brymbo trains. We had half days on Wednesdays and Saturdays: it was a long haul to the station and if I had been detained (detention! – not often, but sometimes) then I did not bother with the Brymbo train but got to the station and went to see if my pals on the Moss Motor were in the bay. If they were, a quiet lift of an eyebrow and I was in a second in the cab. It was cosy on a cold day and platform staff usually had dinner time jobs to do. One delirious moment, when the rail motor had to be moved a few yards for water, and I was allowed to push the regulator open. Bliss!

These little engines so increased passenger traffic especially during high days and holidays that there was a constant stream of traffic going up and down past our house day after day. I had my moments of compunction and felt sorry for drivers and firemen and guards hard at work to make public holidays. My father growled prophecy of trouble to come 'if they over work these willing little engines – you'll see'. And we did see: first one trailer car and then two; we had never heard of any one 'blowing his top' – but my father had, when they sent a rail motor up the steep and twisting branch to Berwig with two trailers. They killed the goose that laid the handy egg!

To Hugh and to me these railmotors were unique in that the two-cylinder engines had Walshaerts valve gear. The driving wheels were coupled. Their exhaust beat was quite different from all other GWR engines of the time: once one had heard an engine with this valve gear, the beat stayed in one's mind!

In the end, Dad proved right. The extra traffic that was generated had to be locomotive worked and the auto train system I have described took over more and more. Up to four coaches – two ahead and two behind the engines could be used. With the rail motors one trailer (passenger car) was the sensible limit.

Chapter 3

Friday and Saturday night trains

Dad used to go to his club one evening of the week. The 'Club' was that backbone of self help in the days before state assistance with such necessities of life as doctors, dentists, medication in sickness and hospitalisation in real illness. My father was an 'Oddfellow', a member of the Manchester Unity of Oddfellows Friendly Society. My grandfather, too was an Oddfellow: after his death the presentation tobacco pipes he had acquired, and many of the jewels of the craft came to Hugh and me in our playroom – which is where active and noisy and spirited children were parked while essential domestic chores went on.

These pipes' shiny red presentation cases made most realistic pistols (don't forget World War One was raging!) and after the battles came the prizes when the Oddfellows Jewels came in handy. As the elder brother, I usually claimed the grandest jewel which became a Victoria Cross in spite of its obvious shape!

But every Friday night, there was a railway ritual that began when my father bought a present for Hugh and me – a North Western train set with a steam engine and three carriages.

He found an old drawing board (a relic of his apprenticeship days) and screwed down on it the usual tin-plate circle of '0' gauge track and a pair of points leading to a station. So on Dad's Club night the locomotive came from its cardboard box and was placed on the rails with its carriages coupled on – then Dad remembered that the tinplate 3 wicks burner had to be filled with methylated spirit. What joy when the cork squeaked out, and the glorious smell of meths quickened our senses. The safety valve was then unscrewed and boiling water poured into the boiler: meantime my mother watched with anxiety as a match was applied to the burners and the engine put back on the rails and coupled to its train.

Acute excitement awaited the first bubble from the cylinders as Dad pushed the loco along. Then more condensate water from the cylinders and off would go the train, Hugh and I safely shepherded by my anxious mother.

When the meths ran out the engine stopped. It was now that Hugh and I were allowed to push the train along the track – and the steam dome was hot and tears resulted.

Later on, we were allowed to play with the train set and the Sambrook children joined in the fun. Eventually, somebody walked on the rails and flattened them; the points were totally wrecked. Such a little addition as station lamps cast in lead remained longer and in the end when I became aware of the damage done in all innocence I grieved mightily. By the time I got under the big dining room table and played at shunting trains of wooden blocks with the wreck of the locomotive – no wheels, no cab, just the boiler – I felt very sad. I got into hot water when I filled the lead station lamp model with paraffin (the lantern had long vanished) – put a bit of string down in and lit it. It was a mourning for glories we had once enjoyed and in ignorance destroyed.

Trains, as you gather, dominated our lives in the Old Vicarage, Brymbo. We went to secondary school by train. Some of us even did our homework on the journey to school – that was a necessity, a chore. Very different was Saturday night excursions to Wrexham.

Saturday night saw complete new trains running up the Minera Branch. In the time when trains ruled supreme, before buses had got a foothold, it seemed to me that hundreds – if not thousands – of our fellows went to Wrexham by train. I remember looking in the early summer nights at a surging mass of people going out of Wrexham Station until I was sure that one could almost walk on the mass of heads leaving the station for the delights of the town. There was money about; the cinema had caught on, the pubs were plenty and popular.

By the time that people were getting back to the station and making for home, the station was seething.

The branches – Brymbo, Moss – normally used two bay platforms, the sign of inferiority, I thought. To meet the heavy Saturday night traffic, Brymbo trains left from the main line up side of the station – in our view the line that led to London-Paddington and the brave new world that beckoned even to us schoolboys.

The usual motor train coaches were not used. We felt the importance of 'proper' compartmented coaches and the long train. We pulled out of Wrexham station agog with all the noise and splendour of the occasion. Through steamed-up windows, we watched as we left the still packed platforms as our heavy train pulled out with the 0-6-0 saddle tank branch engine making the most of the occasion.

We knew, Hugh and I, that with a fully loaded train there might be some excitement. At Southsea, we knew, there might be drama – only of a gentle kind, mind. As the passengers left the train, we'd note that the driver was having a 'blow up' – getting a head of pressure in the engine's boiler for the quite hard climbs to come.

The guard, busy on the platform, would give the 'right away', and Hugh and I would eagerly wait to see how the driver managed. Sometimes the engine had stopped awkwardly and as the driver let his train back a little 'off top dead centre' as Hugh and I knew it, sometimes the engine just stalled from dragging brakes. Then there'd be railway men going up and down under the train and hissing noises as the brake cylinders had to have their pressures, atmospheric and steam, adjusted and reconciled to get the dragging brakes off. We waited, thrilled in gas-lit darkness trying to see what we could while Dad took a knowing look around with a remark to my mother about Jack or Bill or so and so – his old cronies of the days when Brymbo had its own loco shed and there was a chance to take a turn on a footplate some dark and kindly night.

Sooner or later after huffing and puffing, and maybe with a groan of slide bars running a bit dry of oil, we'd be under way. By this time the load was less for stops at Lodge and Brymbo, and the very heavy 1 in 45 pull up to Brymbo West Halt would cause less drama.

Chapter 4

The Minera GWR Branch

The Minera lime quarries were vital to the supply of iron and (later) steel from the Brymbo works.

Minera quarries were the real terminus – C.J. Wignall's invaluable *British Railways Maps and Gazetteer* shows Minera as 'Gds'. The next Halt down the line was Berwig, a place much sought after in the summer which, as I have described elsewhere, maintained in holiday times what seemed to us at Brymbo an unceasing parade of two and three coach passenger trains all day long; so much so that Hugh and I felt sorry for all the drivers, firemen and guards who had to work to make the passengers' holidays. Berwig was a typical GWR Halt; its platform opened out on the country roads to Gwynfryn and Maesmaelor, open moorland and hills. Vicarage Crossing Halt came next and the line continued East to Coed-poeth Station, a typical and lovely red brick station surrounded by cornfields, as I recall, in which I remember the throaty call of the corncrake, now long disappeared, killed off by modern agriculture. In our summer-long holidays from school and Brymbo a great event was Robert Jones' voyage to Coed-poeth Station for coal or farm implements.

From Coed-poeth, the line turned North past Pentre Saeson Halt where Ted Taylor, a friend of my Father's and one of my heroes, had a foundry and ran unusual cars like the Lancia which had no chassis as other cars had but had a sort of steel punt frame to keep its axles and running gear in the right place and had independent front suspension controlled by powerful coil springs. Its engine used only castor oil which gave it the lovely exhaust smell I later learned to associate with the Brooklands track. Ted had a workman who used the castor oil as a medicine: Ted Taylor had an awful fright when the workman, asked to attend to the front suspension had started to unscrew the large nut that held everything in place. 'I just stopped him in time,' he told me. 'If he'd got that nut off the spring might have taken his head off!'

After Pentre Saeson 'Halt for Bwlch-gwyn', the line circled east and dropped down to Brymbo West Crossing Halt and dropped steeply down to Brymbo Station, past the junction with the Mold branch and the Brymbo Steelworks complex of lines after running through the big 4 track crossing controlled by Brymbo Middle Signal Box. I now know that the last drop down to Brymbo station was one of the steepest in Britain's railway system – the last pitch from Brymbo Station to Brymbo West Halt was about 1 in 34, on a twisting line which regularly caused trouble to the Hook Norton iron ore trains and delighted Hugh my brother and me. From our bedroom window we had a grandstand view of heavy trains in trouble on the 1 in 34 banks just a few hundred yards from our window. At the bottom of the steepest bit of line catch points gave an added gravity to the Hook Norton's troubles. Brymbo, of course, was the original station; the Halts were a temporary expedient to combat the growing threat to the railways of electric trams and buses which picked passengers up from the road.

Whenever my mother was expecting a big parcel of winter woollies or blankets from Titley Evans, Llanidloes, the goods would arrive at Brymbo Station; Hugh and I then took a wheelbarrow to bring them home.

The branch that we went to school on took such a circuitous way from Wrexham to Coed-poeth that the distance by road from Coed-poeth to Wrexham was much less – miles less in fact. Once the buses appeared, the passenger traffic on the branch was doomed, although the GWR brought pre 1914 Leyland double deckers with solid tyres in a last effort to counter the threat.

As youngsters, we knew all the traffic movements on the Brymbo Branch, both passenger and goods. The one which we disliked was called the 'Minera Lime' – it woke us up too early, especially during school holidays, coming up to Brymbo about 7.00 a.m. pushing back to Vron Junction and later coming charging down the line to Brymbo West and up to Minera.

During the Royal National Eisteddfod at Mold, the orderly working of Croes Newydd shed was upset – 'specials' from everywhere were running down the 'joint' to Mold, and each had to have a pilot driver on the footplate to show the driver the road. This meant that my friend, Mr Clark, was changed from his usual No. 8 turn to the 'Minera Lime', and his firemen, already a 'passed fireman', was driving on No. 8 turn. From the signalman at Brymbo Middle Box, I received a hint to be on West Halt at 2.15 or so.

Being school holiday, the next day I was there, and the 'Mineral Lime' drew into the Halt, stopped at the starter signal and there was Mr Clark with 1518, an 0.6.0. Pannier Tank Loco. He told me to be on West Halt 7.00 a.m. some morning if I wanted a run up on the Minera Lime and, he said, bring your sandwiches with you.

I went home walking on air and told Mother. I suggested that I would cut the sandwiches that night and cover them with a damp napkin and eat some for breakfast. Mother, being the wonderful person she was, did not agree. She said that I must have a proper breakfast before I go; she got up a some unearthly time, got me out of bed, cooked my breakfast, cut my sandwiches, made me a bottle of tea with lots of sugar, and sent me rejoicing on my way to Brymbo West.

In a short time I saw the Minera Lime approaching Brymbo Station, and the signals came off, the gates at Brymbo Middle opened, and the Minera Lime came storming out of Brymbo Station, taking a run at the steep curve leading to Brymbo Middle and West Halt. Soon she pulled up at the Halt, and I was invited to step up onto the footplate. The signals 'came off' and we pushed back to Vron Junction, over the steelworks crossings under the bridge from the G.C. sidings and into Vron Junction yard.

Here we shunted waggons from Croes Newydd into the steelworks reception siding, picked up two waggons for Caello, backed down onto the rest of the train, the guard coupled up and came to the engine and 'Usual Load: seven of coal and seven empties' and 'One of coal for Caello and two empties'. As soon as the guard reached his van and released the brake, he gave us the right-away. After clearing the steelworks crossings and changing to the line for West Halt, the regulator was opened, and at Middle Box the staff was thrown toward the box. To me, it was a great thrill running down the well-known track at a speed far greater than usual.

At Brymbo West the signalman was holding out the staff and the fireman leaned far out of the cab to take the staff by the loop and swinging round to let the side of the bunker take most of the shock. We had left Vron Junction with the water well up the glass, a good fire and the safety valve blowing off, and now the fire and water needed some attention. The Minera Lime curved and contoured around and along the hillside with a lovely view of Hope Mountain to the right, and Helsby Snout, Beeston Castle and much of the Cheshire Plain in sight. We went past the reservoir supplying water to the High Level tank by Brymbo Middle and the water column and we were approaching Bryn Rhug, a few houses and a foot crossing and the whistle was sounded long and loud. I remember Dr Batty being killed by a passenger train here some two or three years earlier. Shortly after this incident, the driving compartment of the rail motors used on the branch were fitted with the big warning gongs.

Beyond Bryn Rhug the track curved to the left around the shoulder of the hill and here was an occupational crossing and a foot crossing complete with stiles, for which we again whistled long and loud. Shortly after the crossing Caello Brickworks came in sight. From Brymbo West the firemen had worked quietly, 'little and often' with one eye on the water glass and the other on the road. Caello siding was the usual loop holding about 8 or 9 waggons. The driver stopped the train just below the top set and the guard screwed down the van brake, and pinned down some waggon brakes, because of the gradient. The guard came up to the engine, collected the staff, slung it over his shoulder then uncoupled the 'shunt' from the train, came back, stood on the engine step and called out 'One of coal and two empties here, Jack'.

We moved forward, the guard on the step hopping off at the points, and as soon as the waggons were clear stopped us, unlocked the points and called us back. Here we were to pick up waggons on our return journey so we pushed them down away from the wharf and placed our shunt there. The guard uncoupled the waggons, came to the engine and rode on the step until we cleared the points, which he reset and locked, and we returned to the train.

During this shunt I stood in the fireman's corner relaying the guard's hand signals to the driver, while the fireman built up his fire after the hard pull up to Caello, and in anticipation of the curves and gradient from Caello to Coed-poeth, and kept the water well up in the glass. The engine backed down onto the train, the guard coupled up and took off the waggon brakes, got up into his van, and when ready gave us the right-away.

Right hand curve to Caello Crossing, and reverse curve the other side, and a long gentle curve past the fireclay mine (2 waggons on the wharf), on past Smelt Crossing and then to Pentre Saeson Halt and Crossing. Beyond the crossing was the long steep left-hand curve to Gegin Crossing, and beyond that the reverse curve to Coed-poeth Station. Here on the platform to greet us was the station porter, with two empty coal scuttles to be filled with bunker coal, one for the Signal Box and one for the Booking Office.

The starter was a 'calling on' signal, it was off, but the signal protecting the road crossing was on, so we went ahead slowly and waited for a 'hole' in the traffic on the busy Wrexham-Ruthin road to allow us through, then we moved forward to the points to the wharf and warehouse. Here the guard came up for the staff and said, 'Two waggons of coal here, Jack'. We pushed the waggons into the siding, against the wharf, returned to the 'branch', guard reset and locked the points, returned the staff, we backed down on to the train, coupled up, and with 'One of coal for Vicarage Crossing, Jack,' he went back to his van and when ready gave us the right-away.

The crossing was not very far from Coed-poeth, only a matter of 5-6 minutes, with the siding on the Wrexham side of the gates and the halt on the other side. The trouble was that the gates fouled the points, so that to shunt at Vicarage Crossing the road had to be closed. It was not a busy road, fortunately. We stopped short of the crossing, the crossing keeper unlocked and opened the gates, the guard uncoupled the waggon and we pulled clear of the points, which the guard unlocked and set for us to put the 'one of coal' into the siding.

During this shunt I was again in the fireman's corner relaying the guard's hand signals to the driver whilst the fireman coped with fire and water ready for the heavy curves on the way to Berwig Halt. After Vicarage Crossing the line wound round the hillside in a series of tight curves and as we entered the first right hand curve, the wheels started squealing and the engine slowed down, the driver bent down, moved a small lever in front of him, low down, and the noise stopped.

Mr Clark (the driver) explained that the water lubricated the wheel flanges, and that on sharp curves such as these the engine was 'four waggons better' when using the lubricant, and that, usually, only engines so fitted worked the Minera Branch. We were now approaching Berwig Halt, the end of the passenger line; however the Minera Lime works were situated at the bottom of a long gradient leading to the Lime Works down amidst the quarries, and as we approached the end of the line brakes went on and drew us a stop at the entrance to the Lime Works yard. Here, the guard unlocked the points that allowed us access to the yard and prevented the works shunter *Olwen* from running on *GWR* metals. We drew forward, shunted our train into the reception siding as instructed by the works shunter, then down to the Lime Works engine's watering point, filled up with water, built up the fire, shut off the blower and the dampers called it a day, and retired to the cabin snug with its fire lit and ate our sandwiches (mine being warm and with a bit of a hot oil taste about them).

Ivor (the fireman), on finishing his meal left the cabin to see to the fire and I went with him. He opened the fire door, ran the pricker through the fire, opened the dampers, put on the blower and when the fire was bright, he put on a couple of shovels full of selected 'cobbles' and nursed the fire to its normal state, put on the injector and brought the water in the glass up. Satisfied with the result of his labours, we returned to the cabin and reported to the driver 'all's well' and we went out to the engine and started shunting again.

We picked up the five waggon of lime for the steel works and the two empties for Croes Newydd yard. The engine was now working 'bunker first', we backed down onto the van and were ready for the return journey to Brymbo. We moved up to the points which the guard unlocked, forwards through the points, waited for the guard and when he was ready gave us the 'right-away'. Back up the grade we went, to Berwig Halt, where we put the staff in the machine, asked Brymbo West for permission, they accepted us, the staff was withdrawn and handed to the fireman. The gate was opened and we were on our way to Vicarage Crossing, round the curves again with our flange lubricator on and so to Vicarage Crossing. The gates were open, and keeping the loaded lime waggons on the engine went down to the points which the guard unlocked, called us on, picked up the empties for Croes Newydd, and returned to the train. The guard reset and looked the points, we backed up to the train, the guard coupled up and away to Coed-poeth. Here we picked up one waggon and one van for Croes Newydd yard, again hooked on behind the Lime waggons. Held up a few minutes for the road crossing we got away to Coed-poeth Station. Here, the staff was handed to the signalman who, putting it into the machine, passed us on to Brymbo, who accepted us and we had a staff and the line down to Brymbo West.

Before leaving, the guard was given a large and official looking wallet by the booking clerk, then we were passed on to Brymbo. Down over Gegin Crossing to Pentre Saeson Halt and Crossing, stopped to collect another wallet, then on to Caello. Here we picked up four loads of furnace brick, and two empties for Croes Newydd, keeping the Minera Waggons with the engine, so that the waggons for the steelworks could be shunted off at Brymbo Middle. A gentle run round the shoulder of the hill past the crossing, announcing our presence loudly, and soon the signal protecting Brymbo West Crossing came in sight, 'one' holding us up a short while, and the train drew into Brymbo West Halt, and up to the starter, which also was on.

Mr Clark told Ivor that I knew how to use a shovel, so at Coed-poeth on the way up Ivor said, 'No passengers on the footplate' and put the shovel in my hands; the fire was hot and needed little attention so I put a couple of shovelfuls inside the door to cool it a little, and put one shovelful in each corner, and asked him 'How's that?' He took a look at the fire and said, 'Aye that'll do, a bit on the middle perhaps.' I also did a little more before we left Minera, and when I left the engine at Brymbo West, he said, 'So long lad, you can come again' which pleased me and Mr Clark winked at me and laughed.

I walked away from the engine very pleased, rather dirty, hot and sweaty, and walked proudly down the steps and along the lane home, very thrilled and happy, with such a lot to tell Dad, and to thank Mother for.

Chapter 5

Two train journeys

On a hot summer day in 1924, I was sitting in the shade trying to get interested in *Westward Ho*, which was our holiday reading task, when Mother, who was standing on the grass in front of the house called out, 'Mr Clark wants you'.

Mr Clark, who was known to most Brymbo people as Jack Clark, was an engine driver on the *Great Western*, out of Croes Newydd shed and worked No. 8 turn on the Brymbo Branch, usually with pannier tank No. 1824 and George Scott as fireman. Dad knew Mr Clark, who as a young man fired for Jack Jones on No. 772 an 0.6.0. saddle tank loco based in Croes Newydd.

Jack Jones was known as 'Hellfire Jack', a nickname he earned on the popular 9.00 o'clock train from Wrexham to Brymbo on Saturday nights. This train left Wrexham General at the same time as the *GC* train left Central Station also for Brymbo. After leaving Central Station the *GC* Line went under the *GWR* at the Lager Beer Bridge, and this was the last time the trains saw each other until the *GWR* crossed the *GC* at New Broughton, and when they did, the excitement flared up. Sometimes, the GC driver, seeing the *GWR* coming hard up the bank would 'forget' to stop at New Broughton Halt. The stations at Plas Power were side-by-side, and here, urged on by the young bloods on the train, passengers lost no time getting off the train. And now the race was on!

The *GC* had a little longer to run and the curves were sharper, but to even matters the *GWR* had the handicap of a stop at Lodge Halt. Hellfire Jack always started from Plas Power 'like Belle Vue on Bonfire Night', sparks everywhere, high and higher yet in the air. A smart stop at Lodge Halt, a brief stay and Jack was away, then more fireworks as Jack gave 772 everything. Imagine, a train on each side of the valley in sight of each other and going like the hammers, carriage windows full of young and not so young men, shouting taunts across the valley to each other, or encouragement to their respective drivers or just shaking their fists at the other train.

This is the time when bets were being made. The first train into Brymbo Station won, and the driver sounded his whistle long and loud, in triumph. But whoever won, the firemen stood by their engines, ready to accept any token of appreciation that the passenger wished to bestow upon the enginemen. Some people used to complain, but Dad said that most looked forward to it. It made a good and exciting end to the week.

To return to that summer afternoon in 1924. As soon as Mother called out, I ran to the hedge and to my surprise saw Mr Clark 1824 and a train in the background standing at the signal, and before I could say anything he said, 'Come on lad, we're going down the joint to Coed Talon'.

This was really something, I had never been on an engine on the 'joint' as the *GWR* men called it. I was down the yard, over the wall, down the embankment and up on the footplate as quickly as I could, and we were away, over the Prince of Wales Crossing, under Coed-y-felin Bridge, out of the cutting by Brymbo Church and on to the high embankment with a wonderful view of Hope Mountain with the Cheshire Plain to the right and the embankment sweeping gently in a long curve to the left.

It was a 'firemen's dream', fire good and clean after the pull up to Brymbo, water well up in the glass nothing to do except keep one eye on the water and the other on the road. It lasted about 9-10 minutes, then under Pen-y-coed Bridge into the straight that led to Glascoed Viaduct. Now the brakes were applied, and the train slowly crossed the viaduct and stopped with the guard's van nicely clear of it. The guard screwed down his handbrake. We could hear the clink of the pawl as he strained at the last few turns. Coupling pole in hand, he got down and approached the engine. Consulting his book he called out, 'three for the colliery Jack, and two for the silica siding.'

He uncoupled the waggons, collected the staff from George and walked over to the colliery points. We went slowly forward and the guard, with the points now unlocked set then and 'called us on'. We pushed the waggons into the reception siding and the guard 'pinned down' their brakes whilst we went back to the train. Here he joined us, handed the staff back to George, coupled up to the train, walked back to his van, took off the brake and gave us the right-away. We went 'down the joint' for about a quarter of a mile to get to the silica siding. Here the proceedings were similar: van brake on, waggons uncoupled, the guard collected the staff, rode on the step to the points, saw us clear and unlocked and set the points called us on. We pushed the two waggons under the 'silos' and shunted the three loads ready for picking up on our return journey. Again the locking of the points, receiving the staff and returning to the train. As he left the engine the guard called out, 'Three waggons of coal for Llanfynydd, Jack.'

As soon as the guard had given us the right-away, we were off to Llanfynydd, out of the cutting on to the high embankment and on to the high five arched bridge crossing the Nant-y-ffrith valley; from the road I always thought it was a lovely bridge in a wonderful setting, but on this occasion I hung on to the back of coal bunker and was conscious of the long way down. We were soon through Ffrith station and starting to brake for the stop of Llanfynydd. Here we shunted three waggons of coal to one side of the siding, leaving the two empties in a good position for picking up on our return. After this had been completed we got back on to the 'joint', the guard sat and locked the points, coupled us to the train, handed the staff to George, and 'Eight empties for Coed Talon Yard'.

Again it was a perfect trip, completely rural and easy on the firemen and after 10-12 minutes, we saw the signal protecting crossing was 'on' and we had to wait for the road traffic to clear before the gates were opened and we were called forward. We entered the yard, dropped off our waggons, shunted the 'eight of coal' we had to pick up. Now things were very different; the firemen started to work, he did the fire over with the pricker, and started to build up the fire.

This done to the driver's satisfaction, we went and filled up with water, 'trimmed the bunker', me inside with the coal pick, trying to find any lumps hidden under the small stuff, and breaking up any lumps I did find. We backed down on to our train, moved out on to the 'joint' again and waited for the signal which soon gave us the road, and we left Coed Talon for the return trip to Brymbo. Up to Llanfynydd it was an easy trip, George firing on the 'little and often' system. We got to Llanfynydd in 10-12 minutes and picked up our three empties. Then away for the Silica sidings where we picked up our three loads for Lever Bros; onward to the Glascoed Colliery siding.

Here we had an argument. The guard wanted to pick up all three waggons, but the driver didn't want to hang on any more, as he considered we were close to the maximum load, and if they put another three on and the engine failed for any reason, then he would have to take a walk to the shedmaster's office, a thing he did not want to do at any price. The argument continued, not at all nasty, and we had to laugh at many of the sallies.

To satisfy the colliery people and 'to show willing', as the guard put it, the driver agreed to take one. Now all the usual moves were made: he took the staff, unlocked the points, set them for us to go into the reception siding after it was uncoupled, eased one waggon of coal down until it cleared the points, pinned down the waggon brakes, reset the points to let us out of the siding and we dropped down, gently, to the waggon, coupled up and then dropped down to the train and the guard coupled us to the rest of the train, then came up to the engine, handed the staff and said, 'Nine loads coal, two silica, and three empties'.

During the whole of this time George had been busy with fire and water. The colliery siding was just beyond the big curve where the line left the Glascoed Viaduct so that we had no chance of a run at what was to come. As soon as we got the right-away from the guard and the train nicely on the move, the lever went down to the bottom of the quadrant and the regulator right over to the stop and with the steam roaring at the safety-valve we were on the viaduct.

Since leaving Coed Talon the engine had been running bunker first, the driver with his left hand on the cab side his back to the boiler and his right hand hovering over the regulator, watching the road over the bunker. He shouted to me, 'Tell me when we come to the foot crossings' then, without saying anything to George, reached over for the lever working the fire-box doors and started an exhibition of 'joint working'.

The fireman's shovel went into the bunker, and as it came out the driver opened the firehole doors, the empty shovel withdrawn, the fire-box doors slammed shut, the shovel back to the bunker, a continuous effort of almost mechanical precision, quite ballet-like in its perfection. The effort of the engine was terrific, you could feel it – in the thump of the pistons, the kick of the lever against the stops the blast and the roll, the whole atmosphere on the footplate was one of 'battle stations'. I indicated when the footpaths were near, and twice the whistle was blown without a break in the 'ballet'. The blast from the chimney, the roar of the blower and the general footplate noises made speech impossible but I noticed that there was still a whisp of steam at the safety-valve as we came up to Pen-y-coed Bridge.

I had not realised how great the blast really was, and once under the bridge it hit us. I expected the bridge to be blown off its foundations, or at least a few coping stones around our ears, and was glad it was a bridge and not a tunnel.

Once past the bridge a combination of curve and bank began to slow 1824 down, and anxious glances were cast at the glass, but 1824 still kept hard at it, and once round the curve and with the fixed distant signal, protecting Prince of Wales Crossing in sight, the end of the hard work was also in sight. The firing now stopped, the injector put on and a long blast alerted the Prince of Wales Crossing keeper that we were on our way, and coming up to Coed-y-felin Bridge we were relieved to see the signal was off. Once through the Crossing, steam was shut off, and speed soon fell to a walking pace and I was able to step down from the engine step safely into the 'six foot'.

After seeing me safely on my feet a toot on the whistle and a wave from the cab, the train resumed its journey to Brymbo Station and Croes Newydd and I, still excited, hot and dirty after my efforts in the bunker, but happy and grateful to my kindly 'Knights of the Footplate' for such a wonderful experience.

* * *

We went as a family in 1921 by train from Brymbo to Mountain Ash and it made a memorable journey. We didn't know it; but it was the end of much heavy industry in Wales. From Wrexham we passed through the edges of the North Wales coalfield. In Mountain Ash, Margaret's sleep was disturbed by what she thought were 'big fires burning along the tops of the mountains'. It was Dowlais Steelworks' blazing furnaces lighting up the night sky. George Borrows described it many years before this. Later in life, as a journalist, I attended a meeting at which the end of the Dowlais works was announced: there would be no more light on the mountain tops. Indeed, most of industrial Wales was to be 'blacked out'.

The railway journey was a panorama of the Welsh Valleys – from Pontypool Road the timetable reads 'Crumlin High Level, Tredegar Road, Rhymny Junction, Llancaiach, Treharris, Quakers' Yard, Penrhiwceiber, Mountain Ash'.

The great moment to us children came when our train pulled out on to that remarkable viaduct, the Crumlin Bridge. We gazed spell-bound through the carriage windows at the tiny houses below, diminished by distance, as were roads, railways, farms, animals and people, and we sank back into the safety of our seats.

My father loved every mile of a train journey. He had absorbed railway lore from his many railway friends. To my mother's anxiety he was always preoccupied by the operational minutiae of a train journey. The guard, for example, must always be on a passenger train: a good guard looks back to see that all is well with the train as it leaves a station. So when Dad, looking back as the train left the station before the Crumlin Bridge saw the guard fail to board the train and left a swinging door as he fell back, immediately did his duty and pulled the

Communication Cord. We children, of course had instant visions of policemen, jails and the sudden end of our world. The driver managed to keep his train going in spite of the emergency brake application. Dad, of course had been half out of his window all the time. Cowering in our seats we heard an official voice: 'Was it you who gave the alarm?'

Dad was now out on the platform and we heard snatches of conversation, and, finally, a uniformed head appeared at the window and we heard a voice saying to Mother: 'Thank you, Ma'am; your husband did us a good deed, and we're very grateful!' So ended the story of the Crumlin Bridge.

But not quite, this bridge was made of open work girders, since its designers fear for the stability of a masonry structure because of the high winds that funnelled past the site. Like the original Britannia Bridge over the Menai Straits it was made of wrought iron and it had been decided that it was worth preserving. Because of the distance across the valley, a wooden walkway had been built below the rails across the valley. Some years ago I was idly watching a film – a James Bond one, I think, with some luscious film star doing impossible heroics. They were caught on a bridge across a valley and were being machine gunned from a helicopter. I stared in disbelief – but it *was* the Crumlin Bridge! Needless to say, but yes – by some mischance – it, too, was demolished.

Chapter 6

Roads

A public house stood opposite the Old Vicarage – indeed, still stands. It is called *The Railway Inn*.

The left hand extension of Railway Road dropped down quite steeply to a little shopping area: Tommy Sims' shop, Grainger's greengrocer and China; very modest – and Britner the Barber's long low wooden shop, considered by our parents unsuitable for small boys. It had a wonderful smell of newspapers and *Woodbines* and something that even my innocence felt sophisticated in a way I could not understand.

On the opposite side of the road to Britner's newsagency there was a mysterious shell of a building that had no windows. It was being built by the go-ahead Grainger family. I had been sent down by my mother for some plaice. (I was fascinated by Harry Grainger's dexterity in slicing fish from the skin with a very sharp knife.) I asked Mrs Grainger about the new building and she took me across the road to see it. Probably it seemed easier than trying to explain what 'moving pictures' were to a curious small boy!

Mrs Grainger's son George was a motorcyclist who had an immaculate 1914 belt-drive BSA which he converted to a more modern chain drive himself. It needed a 'cush-drive' hub in the rear wheel and so tended to tear out spokes. Later on he bought a Stuart-Turner petrol engine and a dynamo and charged up the 'wet' batteries of our wireless sets. There was no electricity supply in Brymbo.

Opposite Britner's shop a road branched off left through Brymbo Green to Halcog, passing the *Queen* public house, from it a road led right here passing small whitewashed cottages in one of which lived the Fried Fish Shop owners; the chip shop was typically primitive, a coal-fired range. For a penny you got chips wrapped in a sheet of newspaper. Hugh or I was given a china bowl and a few coppers and sent for chips. The bowl was given to the chip shop man to be heated – and we waited, and waited. When our turn came it was a quick dash home with a couple of surreptitious chips extracted from the bowl on the way!

From the chip shop the road carried on through Station Road and over to Brynteg and Moss passing the Brake Tunnel, Major Brown's Colliery and Moss Halt on the *GWR* Moss Branch.

From Britner's shop the 'main' Brymbo road passed a pub we knew as *The Tai Inn*; opposite a small primitive *tŷ a siamber* – a single storey house with a second 'chamber' built on.

The road carried on towards the Tai bridge which carried the Mold-Brymbo (*LNWR*) and the Wrexham-Minera lines over it. It turned left after going under the bridge, climbed towards Brymbo Station on its left and Bethel (Welsh) Wesleyan on its right. Past the chapel the road dropped steeply down to the Lodge, then quite a village. It was wiped out with the growth of the steelworks embankment and once gave shelter to the other Brymbo Station, that of the *Great Central Railway* which had made a bid for a share in the traffic arising from the Brymbo area's minerals and finished iron and, later, steel products. I do remember that the *GCR* Brymbo passenger service ended in 1917: station-master Miller was transferred to Sandy in Bedfordshire after the 1921 strike.

Before organised bus services ran to Brymbo several Model T Fords ran passengers to King Street, Wrexham (before the bus station opened there). As I remember the fare one way to Wrexham was four pence. I remember a woman driver of a Model T: she had a vast leather overcoat, and the canvas hooded car had side curtains fastened with the first zip-fastener I ever saw.

My first recollection of Bethel was that it had been part of a small hamlet skirting the then much less threatening steel- works bank. From Bethel the road led downhill past the Tai Bridge and climbed alongside the railway embankment to Brymbo, passing a few houses and the Public Hall on its left: it then dived under the very low bridge that carried the *GWR* tracks to the steelworks.

The bridge was the Mount Bridge – the *Mount Hotel* was just a little further on the right – and it figured largely in Dad's stories of his younger days when the new bicycling craze hit Brymbo. The newer 'safety' bikes had replaced the old 'penny-farthings' and, Brymbo being a hilly village with winding roads and tricky bends, the local 'Mashers' had devised a sort of race circuit. Their exploits on this speed track had got to the ears of the sporty boys of our nearest neighbouring village – Coed-poeth. Instant rivalry burned in the breasts of the Coed-poeth *'ufferns'*. (*Uffern* is the Welsh word for the Nether regions, so I need not elaborate on the epithet.)

Finally, a contest was arranged, and it so happened that the chosen route led down a steepish little drop from Harwd Road into the dark tunnel-like entrance to the long, low, Mount Bridge. The Brymbo team was mounted on the new low safety bikes. The Coed-poeth men had their penny farthings and loudly announced the speed their big driving wheels would allow. Now the rider on his penny farthing stood – or sat! – too high by virtue of his big front wheel to pass through the lowest part of the Mount Bridge . . .

The Public Hall was much used in the darker days of the Great War, and here I first heard 'We'll Keep the Home Fires Burning', 'Pack up your troubles in your old kit bag', and 'Goodbye, Dolly Gray' – although that was a throw back to the other war – the Boer War. Freddie Hughes, son of the keepers of the *Railway Inn* and I got into hot water when we went around Brymbo Green singing another throw back to the Boer War –

> 'Poor old Kruger's dead
> He died last night in bed,
> Buy a penny roll
> Stick it up his . . .
> Poor old Kruger's dead.'

I have no conception of where I acquired this rude ditty from. The consequences made sitting down an ordeal for a day or so . . .

My mother had one endearing habit. If anything really amused her she would laugh until tears streamed down her face. That happened as I overheard my parents discussing my rude ditty.

When later I took a chance and told her I'd heard her laughing over it, her excuse was that it reminded her of an incident during her district training in Canton, Cardiff. She did her usual athletic leap on to a moving tramcar and she got a piece of grit in her eye and sat on a corner seat to use her hankie, another passenger put an arm on her shoulder and said, 'Don't cry, Nursie, the Boers have just about had enough fighting and I'm sure he'll be home again, safe and sound, before much longer!'

Major Brown was a trim, sparse, military type who was in our morning school train when we joined it at Brymbo West. He left the train at Brymbo Station, and as he walked up to his colliery he could not fail to see what his Yorkshire steam waggon was doing to Brymbo Roads. This was before tarmac was widely used and all our roads were the old water-bound macadam invented for country roads and horse drawn traffic. Major Brown's waggon carried I suppose about 10 tons of coal on its steel wheels with massive steel treads across the wheels. It came down laden from his colliery, on the steep narrow road past Brymbo Station, over the level crossing and down past Bethel Chapel and steeply up to the *GWR* Goods Station, where it filled railway waggons with coal.

I vividly remember Hugh and I being taken home from a tea-party at Bethel and being confronted by the terrifying colossus that was Major Brown's! In wet weather it ploughed huge craters in the road that were impossible for our short legs to get over. Imagine a small child's panic, islanded in a massive, muddy, steel wheel created rut in the road, hearing afar the crashing sound of the steam waggon's approach.

Hugh and I knew about steam boilers and safety valves. We had watched the stoker of the traction engine, faced with the steep hill back to Black Lane Colliery and conscious of falling boiler pressure, as it waited for the crossing gates outside Brymbo Station, take a heavy hammer and clout the safety valve.

As far as we knew it never blew up, but . . .

Years later I think I saw its rusting hulk still in the *GWR* Goods yard. I don't think it ever blew up!

* * *

It was before *Walls* ice-cream came to Brymbo; we kept watch on Tommy Sims' shop about half-past eight, (by this time Brymbo had buses to Wrexham). If we saw Tommy with a roll of sacking under his arm we knew he was bound for the *Lager Beer* works in Wrexham and that he would return with a block of ice. His machine he then filled with chopped ice and salt in a wooden pail which held a menial cylinder charged with ice-cream powder and water which was rotated by a handle. The 'ice-cream' it made was scooped out and spread (not thickly enough for us) on a wafer on a metal platen, another wafer on top, a twist of a spring and the (very slim) ice-cream wafer was ours. Two pence, and three pence for a large one, as I recall.

Tommy Sims' small shop window drew us with its display of toffees and sweets: inside the shop Tommy sliced bacon from round filches with a very sharp knife: the shop sold all the food Brymbo Green shoppers needed. But after the shop shut it became a focus of attraction for the young men in that it rivalled Britners barber's shop which I have previously noted.

I am told that the fraternity which assembled there after hours kept an eye on the Charles (Old Vicarage) house and Tommy would observe 'Time up lads – the Charles family have put their lights out.'

In our young days, Harrison's Cambrian Stores and Brymbo Co-op were our main shops. Mrs Harrison carried the last of a fading business, a solitary old lady, bent with age, specs on the end of her nose, a knitted house coat tight over her thin shoulders . . . once filled shelves now tricked out with cardboard sample packets tired and dirty from long handling...new holes in the floorboards and decay.

Its next move was to become the offices of the Brymbo Water Company, and the attached house became my home.

* * *

Just after the war the Harrison's shop was apparently prosperous: I think it was the sort of corner-shop trade that was so prized before the black depression of the 30s ruined them. Mrs Harrison was a frail widow with a rusty-black shawl round her old bent shoulders that typified her. The shop had once been a very good, profitable business I heard my mother and father say: there was another Harrison shop across the hill in Broughton. It was here we came in the hot 1917 and 1918 summers to bet *burum* – 'balms' essential to make 'real' lemonade. This started in a big Buckley Brownstone vessel that we called a 'panmug'. It was much used in farms for collecting and storing milk. On the outside it was a rough brown pottery: the inside was brightly glazed.

Into it would go many lemons, lots of boiling water, lots of sugar cubes and of course balm. The panmug was then left to cool and covered with a clean white cloth.

I do not know how long it stayed in the panmug: I do know that surreptitious tastings of a finger ventured into the panmug when all backs were turned were disappointing. But the day came when my mother or Nain Margaret – an old family retainer – pronounced the brew was ready and my father was called in. The liquid was bottled and corks pressed in and tied down quite firmly. Then the bottles were taken to the cool dairy to await the call. Pressures were high inside the bottles. In 1921, when my mother had an urgent call to her family in Mountain Ash, Dad got Thomas Alfred to take her to Shrewsbury with his car. The only viable connection was by *North Western* train from Shrewsbury to Pontypool Road and change there to the Neath line which ran through Mountain Ash. A tedious journey. We were waiting his return, the one remaining bottle of lemonade much in our thoughts. To our horror, as Dad picked it up to do the ceremonial uncorking it blew up in his hand. My sister Margaret, then five years old remembered her disappointment for years!

For some obscure reason my recalling 'panmugs' reminded me of some of the unwelcome but necessary chores that fell to our lot. Knives were simple steel in those days – and they rusted overnight. Anyone who left a knife on a vinegary plate at supper awoke to a telling off next morning. The only way to clean knives was with a large cork and bath-brick: a coarse stone easily broken down into a polishing medium. With a couple of drops of water on the bathbrick, cork into the mixture, and you literally had to grind out the rust from the blade. Given that knives were kept sharp, any careless conjunction of knife, cork and bathbrick meant a gashed finger.

My father's elder sister had married a steelman engaged in coke and chemical products and had moved to Sheffield. He came over to Brymbo and brought us a set of the latest wonder – stainless steel knives that *never* rusted! We blessed his name and the genius of Sheffield.

* * *

Many a morning in the bleak, early light in which we got ready for breakfast and school there would come a timid knock on the kitchen door. It was usually a grubby but polite, small (very small at times) child offering a small exercise book. It was a high door step and it would mean bending right down to reach the child's hand. There was little need to read the message: it asked for help and never expected more than pence. Dad, without a word would give a silver sixpence piece and sign the book. Usually it was to help pay some unexpected demand: most often a funeral. Today that would be remarkable: in those hard times it was commonplace. Men died in the pits and widows received a few pounds to tide them and their family over the crisis. This too was the time of the 'tontine' a fund for some family need. Mostly it was done at work or in the pubs, and always at Christmas there would be bitter and sorrowful stories of an anxious 'investor' going to the club or pub on the share-out night and finding that the do-gooder had decamped with the proceeds. No share-out; tragedy.

When hard times came during strikes, or as when Brymbo Steelworks shut down for three years, a different system ruled. Chapel men and women and church men and women got together and organised 'craft-centres', very different from today's craft centres. Premises were found, and there men would find tools, lasts, nails and shoe leather all set out ready to put soles and heels on children's shoes. There were no 'Wellington boots' or 'quick reach-me-downs' then: I cannot recall any child in really bad boots during school. These premises were usually older houses not occupied. I remember some such in old cottages with cardboarded broken windows and two – wick paraffin 'heaters'.

* * *

We had to go to Lodge if we wanted to consult a doctor. If you were ill enough to need hospital treatment the place was Wrexham Infirmary. My father, mother, brother and I one summer evening went for a walk after Chapel to our 'scouting ground' which gave us scope to be cowboys or British tommies fighting the Germans (by the way many toys came from Germany and were stamped with the letters 'D.R.G.M.' which no doubt echoed Deutschland in its make-up; our translation of it was 'Dirty Rotten German Made' – in spite of the fact that (unknown to us) many of the model steam engines came from Bing and they even produced models of British steam locomotives sold by Bassett-Lowke as their own make!)

Disaster struck on one Sunday after chapel walk on the edge of our scouting ground. My mother stepped on a leaf while crossing a stile; her foot slipped and she fell with all her weight on one knee. She was holding on to a barbed wire fence and cut her hand quite badly. Messages were got to Thomas Alfred and he brought his model T Ford around and my mother was taken home. It was obvious that something serious had happened to her knee (she had broken her knee-cap) and I had a very distressful night watching over her: she was in much pain and I almost fainted in sympathy. Next time I saw her was in the Wrexham Infirmary, a stark and severe Victorian building which, when the War Memorial Hospital was built, housed the burgeoning Technical Institute. This was my first visit to a hospital and the lasting impression I got, as a visitor, not as a patient, was of stark coldness, cold white beds, iron bed frames and an almost Dickensian feel of rectitude.

It was financed by public subscription and the Secretary of the Hospital was Leslie Spencer, and my brother-in-law Jimmy Dryburgh came from a Wallasey hospital as his assistant.

He married my sister Margaret who later took charge of Meadowslea TB Hospital, the Welsh National Memorial Association of which Lord Davies of Llandinam was a generous patron. Jimmy Dryburgh went on to be treasurer of Clwyd Health Authority and he and Margaret, after moving to Llangernyw, did yeoman work in training and enthusing village children to become proficient in Red Cross Work.

One visit to an early X-ray installation left me with vivid memories. I was twelve and in some schoolboy frolic had hurt my back. Our doctor said an X-ray was necessary. I think it was in Temple Row in Wrexham:

all I can remember was lots of wires and when the plate was being exposed a huge spark gap that crackled and hissed (and, since I had been to Grove Park Chem Labs, and knew the smell) quite made me dizzy with what I thought was ozone produced by the spark gap!

Chapter 7

Summer Holidays

Our whole family benefited from the Brymbo Water Company's mountain possessions – reservoirs, lakes, mountains, filter-houses and the like. Pendinas reservoir was more of a lake above the Bwlch-gwyn – Llandegla Road on Maes Maelor.

The main filter house looked just like a chapel, except for its big front doors. It was cool on the hottest summer day; its steel bodied filter chambers seemed big to us, and suitably like an ocean liner's engine room. Pumps hissed and clanked and there were exciting noises when the filter beds had to be washed. There were parts of the filter house which made ideal tables for picnic feeds: a big white-washed fireplace even made smoke-flavoured tea from a big iron kettle. All summer we were surrounded by moorland which grew the loveliest, juiciest whinberries.

During all the 1914-1918 war we children and my mother went as soon as school broke up for the summer holidays to the country.

We fell in love with a farm – Pen Lan – on a small hill above the Bwlch-gwyn – Llandegla Road – we called it Maes Maelor; others knew it as the Denbigh Moors, or Hiraethog in Welsh.

Dad got Thomas Alfred to bring his Model T Ford round when Brymbo school closed for the summer and everything needed went into it. I am ashamed to remember that we fled so quickly that I can remember coming back when school started and finding my discarded vest and underpants just as I had left them in the scramble to get away! It took a weekend to settle in. Dad came with us, but once he had seen us safely in our beds he'd go back to Brymbo. At weekends he caught the Coed-poeth branch line train to Berwig Halt and walked over the old road from Gwynfryn. He loved walking and enjoyed the break.

Pen Lan was in two parts – a modern brick building and a much older, probably original, farm house.

'Visitors' had the more modern part, and we all three – Hugh, my sister Margaret, born in August 1916, and I – enjoyed the freedom and the novelty of farm life. The family in the farm were three – Robert Jones and his two sisters. One was plump and jolly, the other sister leaner. As with all girls of the time they had gone 'out to service' as soon as they were old enough after leaving school – both were very kind to us children. The farm bordered on the open mountain, and a small brook ran along the boundary with the open mountain and supplied the farm with water. A small yard lay in front of the house; on its left some plum trees and a field through which the lane went to the main road over a small but lively stream.

The farm buildings were a small set of rough stone buildings: nearest the house a barn with a chaff-cutter and a few tools; next to it a cow house with a hay loft above; then Darby's stable – a handsome mare and provider of all the horsepower the farm boasted; a gate separated the buildings from the stackyard. From the farm yard wall, a rough and quite steep path led down to a wooden bridge across the small stream in a field whose gate opened on to the main road. Across the road a gate opened on to a small track that led up into a gully which climbed steeply into the open mountain. There was a small cottage just inside the road gate: we called it Hafod-dafolog: it would have been much sought after to make a holiday home today. It had a pleasant look and oriel windows let into the roof, Scottish fashion. Its only signs of life were many swallows' mud nests under the eaves. Each year we went there, the house diminished: I think that by the end of the 1914-18 war it had largely disappeared.

There was much of the old landlordism left. We were solemnly warned not to go on to the open moorland or mountain after the sacred twelfth of August when the shooting started: the 'goback-goback' cry of the grouse was still heard and a very occasional pheasant came surreptitiously our way, to be eaten with gusto until our teeth jarred on the lead shot that we were warned about but had forgotten in the novelty of the occasion. We heard the guns; neighbouring farmers gossiped about y byddigions – the grand people, the guests of the estate owners.

Farming in Wales had not yet fallen into the 'dog and stick' era that came after the war, Pen Lan saw corn harvests and we watched with admiration when Robert Jones thatched his stacks with reeds from the river bed pushed in bundles into the stack with split wooden pegs to keep the thatch water-tight. We got to know the few Irish farm hands who came into the area to help out with harvesting. One man, Jack Larkin by name, came every year. He once fell on a scythe blade and cut his hand badly. Mama looked after it until it healed (without stitches!) and – as couple of blankets (the cart had iron tyres and no springs, and tarmac was unheard of). What saved our bodies, I now realise, was Darby, the cart-horse: her pace was a quiet amble. It didn't distress us too much.

The other event was the result of one of the milking cows, normally quiet, starting to make a lot of noise around the farm. '*Gofyn tarw*,' said Robert Jones, when I asked why she was mooing all the time. He wouldn't elaborate, and when I asked his sisters I got the same look on their faces which told me plainly that I had ventured into that family minefield which led to discussions of babies and odd looks and sudden silences.

I can now realise what a problem this presented to a bachelor farmer and his two spinster sisters. And to my parents, for the cow was 'bulling': the Welsh *gofyn tarw* said it more succinctly – 'She wants the bull'.

Obviously the decision was made, for Robert Jones, we three children and the cow walked to a neighbouring farm, the cow met the bull briefly and back we came to Pen Lan, very puzzled. It was explained by my mother that the cow would now have a calf. We couldn't credit it. 'Just by jumping on her back – that's all?' we queried. There was much mystery, but no further discussion. Years later we understood.

The two Miss Joneses in Pen Lan had both worked in the houses of Victorian and Georgian worthies in the Wirral peninsula. One claimed, I think, to have worked for John Bright; the other had an interesting series of stories about her adopted Merseyside, and told us of a factory where long trains of orange peel came, and where machines made pips for raspberry jam out of wood. Both were cooks of much experience, and we benefited much from our summer holidays.

One year during a long, hot summer and an August which brought meadows full of mushrooms brought also a coal strike. Many out of work colliers came walking along our roads and had a glad harvest of mushrooms. We had them cooked by experts, with real home-cured bacon – hanging, traditionally, like pictures from the beams in the kitchen. Farm bacon and farm eggs and fresh farm milk – and mushrooms!

During the hard rationing of the 1914-18 war the rabbits of Maes Maelor were much in demand and it was noteworthy how in the days when only bicycles and feet provided transport the petrol engine wrought wonders. First motor-bikes; then came the days of the big Triumphs and the AJS and BSA machines. Soon they added side-cars, and the countryside began quietly to prosper. Along roads that once had know nothing much except the houses made memorable by the old names – '*Casgan Ditw, Tafarn y Gath, Llety Llygoden a Brandy Bach*' new red she often did if anything really funny tickled her – laughed until tears ran down her face as Larkin tried to pronounce the name of the town he was due to walk to for his next job – 'Pwllheli'.

As you can imagine we found lots to do. Hugh and I took over the rabbit snares; Robert Jones showed us the runs which he snared with loops of thin wire attached to pegs pushed into the ground. It was our first experience of death at first hand, and we saw how the light went out of a rabbit's eye as Robert Jones took it out of the snare and hit it with the side of his hand behind the rabbit's head. Eyes that had been bright and alive in life, glazed over and were lightless as it died.

One thing we discovered in Pen Lan – in a musty old cupboard in the oldest part of the house we found a copy of the first *Hopalong Cassidy* book to have been published. In it Clarence E. Mulford, its author (I have an idea he had never been near the cow-punching West) made the mistake of letting Hopalong get married to Mary Meeker. We entered the saga while Hopalong roamed the West trying to forget his Mary (after the author had decided to kill her off) and earning his creator and publisher much money. But it was full of guns and gun craft and since our visits with Dad to his LDV shooting range with bored-down Lee Enfield .303 rifles, we had taken quite a fancy to guns.

Also in the older part of the farmhouse was the dairy. All milking was by hand: we did venture, but were not won over. I was pressed however into churning with an old end-over-end churn. As with most people I grew to dislike it heartily! How often I looked into the little glass window smeared with the products of my labour which seemed endlessly useless; – never butter!

But I hated farm butter – *menyn ffres* as it was called at home. 'Fresh' butter to me meant what Percy Tunley in Brymbo Co-op produced with two wooden 'pats' and much skill from a solid mass of butter on a marble slab on the butter counter. In the end I was given margarine – not the sort we get today, but a waxy tasteless substance. I used to put mustard on it to get at least some taste!

The great disadvantage about Pen Lan to as avid a reader as I was in those days was the long, dusty, empty road that I had to walk in the July and August heat to get my *Children's Newspaper* (Arthur Mee's) or my *Meccano Magazine*. Dad brought a week's *Daily Post* and my mother's magazines up at weekends. I couldn't wait that long – hence the route march.

There were memorable excursions along that same road, though. Once or twice Robert Jones had to go to Coed-poeth Station for coal. This was a major event. Old sacks on the cart floor instead of cushions, a brick houses – yes, one could call them 'villas' – sprang up along the roadside. The town had discovered the countryside and its larder-enhancing possibilities.

Chapter 8

School Days

But holidays came to an end and it was back to school.

Brymbo Council School was a beacon of modern ideas in an otherwise mediocre Victorian Board School Service. Denbighshire established council schools – and in Brymbo, at least, the new school outshone the old Church School as well.

I know my grandfather was influential in providing in Brymbo Council School a model building. Brymbo had no electricity or gas. Brymbo Council School had gas. Each week a big petrol lorry would drive down the steep road from the imposing main entrance to a peculiar tall narrow building between the girl's playground and ours. There it unloaded what seemed to us boys to be dozens of the usual two-gallon screw stoppered cans. To undo the brass cap that sealed the tin you used the stiff steel weld on the bottom corner of the tin, engaged the lugs on the brass cap – a twist of the wrist and you filled the tank. But this was not easy; you had to pour the petrol with the off-set cap pointed upwards – or you'd soak your shoes and trouser bottoms!

But – gas in the new school. Mr Edwards the caretaker came and wound and wound on a big handle that raised a large weight – probably accounting for the high narrow building. The whole school was lit by gas: it had a modern domestic science block which modelled a family home, and had a laundry with gas heaters for the smoothing irons. For years my mother stuck her irons in front of the red-hot bars of the 'Excelsior' range until dad found a modern looking gas iron with a round plated ball behind the handle. You filled the ball with petrol, put back the screw top which had a one-way valve in it, pumped up the pressure, put in a little meths, a match – and on with the ironing!

One notable peculiarity about my Brymbo school was the almost exclusive use of the English language in the school. True, there was a passing regard to Wales in that busts of Tom Ellis and Owen Edwards stood on the wall of the Central Hall. Tim Selby, the headmaster was a monoglot Englishman and a churchman. I remember one Welsh speaking assistant teacher, a Miss Williams, I think, from Tanyfron. It was she who taught my class, standard Three, I think, to sing *'Wrth fynd efo Deio i Dywyn'*, and I am grateful that later on I was taught to sing Dafydd y Garreg Wen's dying lament.

I went to school when I was three – in 1912 – and I have the memory of a remarkable assistant teacher who drew in chalk on the floor of the hall of the infant school a diagram of the Dardanelles campaign in which members of my mother's Mountain Ash family were involved. Her cousin Sophie Britton lost her husband in Churchill's attempt to plunge a knife into the 'soft underbelly' of the Kaiser's alliance. My sister Margaret owed her second name to the battle, however: Hugh and I had been sent to Mountain Ash for her birth and we were summoned to my great aunt's knee and told of her arrival. At the request that we help find her a name we decided on Elizabeth, for, to us, the ample reason that the battleship Queen Elizabeth, with her 14 inch guns, could shoot her 14 inch projectiles clear over hills to harry the Turks 14 miles away. Second Liet. Britton was wounded and was thought to have died when the Turks set fire to masses of brushwood which killed many of the wounded. Sophie had to live the rest of her life a widow of a soldier she did not know beyond doubt was dead.

The other all-important influence on my life was Bethel Chapel, but time moved on for Bethel, too. When I came home from some job that had taken me away from Brymbo I drove my car the well-known way to where Bethel was. It had disappeared. Completely. All I found on the site was an ornamental six-inch piece of what I recognised as the railings around the front door.

All I ever wanted to be apart from an engine driver or a racing motorist was a writer. In Brymbo council school when I was in Standard 4 there was a young woman teacher who one day marked an essay of mine in which I had tried to use a word which I knew – or felt – meant 'sudden, harsh'. I wrote 'abrute', and was covered in confusion when she asked me to explain what I meant. She was a teacher of some genius: she knew just what I wanted to say, and suggested 'abrupt'. The very sound of the word as she spoke it conveyed exactly my meaning.

About the same time we had a young teacher called – if I remember correctly – Arthur Morgan. He lived in Lodge, Brymbo and had, I think, just been demobbed (from World War One – I knew this because like so many of our teachers he wore a khaki tie, khaki socks and other evidence that he had not long been wearing civilian dress). He brought into class for us, for an English lesson a slim booklet which astonished me with such phrases as 'the rough male kiss of blankets', and 'the warm crust of friendly bread'. Who wrote them I don't know, but words suddenly became important to me. I loved them; I felt them on my tongue.

My mother loved books and read a lot. She passed that love on to me. After a childish ailment – a cold, or scarlet fever, when I was convalescent she would put me in a big, comfortable chair in front of the sitting room fire and give me a book to read. I can remember *Robinson Crusoe, The Swiss Family Robinson, Ivanhoe* and a series of spell-binding novels by an American Gene Stratton-Porter, with stories of the American middle west *Freckles, Girl of the Limberlost* and others.

So much I owe to some of my teachers; in my years in Grove Park County School, Wrexham, my admiration goes to another man, not long demobbed, who also wore khaki shirts and collars and ties. He had found a German exponent of Shakespeare when Bradley was all the rage here. It was he who told me in a smoke-filled staffroom one morning: 'Charles, you can write. What are you going to do about it?' He found the post-graduate courses in journalism for me, which put me on the road to achieving some little ambitions I treasured.

G.B. Harrison, a noted Shakespeare scholar, was my tutor in Kings College, London. He asked me to review what I saw as the development of Macbeth's character after the death of Banquo. He read my essay in silence and then asked, 'What school did you go to?' 'Who taught English there?' I had to explain to him what a 'County' school was, but he was very impressed by what Bob Andrews had taught me about Shakespeare.

Another man I am indebted to was Jonathan Jones, a Maths master, whose taste in transport appealed to me and who read *Autocar, Motor and Light Car* and *Cyclecar* every week. He had a motorcycle combination called 'Seal' (it stood for Sociability, Ease And Lightness, I found); the driver sat in the sidecar and there was some wet-weather protection. After a terrifying annual examination when I scored 11 out of 400 in Maths, and was faced with a career in an accountant's office since one had to have Maths to Matriculate and get to University, Jonathan offered me a deal – he would work three months with me if I worked with him. He made it all so understandable that I passed London Matric's First Division and so went to King's College in London.

The surprising thing is that he did not teach Maths – why I can't remember. By chance he judged the School Eisteddfod Model Competition in which I had entered a model of a Guy motor-bus chassis. Because of the limitations of the Meccano system I could not model the three speed forward and reverse gearbox correctly and put in a note to explain why. I was delighted to get a first prize – but I got with it a letter from Jonathan Jones explaining that he'd adjudicated the competition before reading my letter, and invited me to see him. Another smoke-filled staffroom!

He remarked that he had no idea that my interest lay in engines and science. He knew of my acute problem with Maths and was sporting enough to offer to help. That is why, although my ambition were set on becoming a journalist, I felt how fulfilling a job teaching could be, as I well knew from my own experience!

Chapter 9

Coal

The very name Brymbo comes from coal – or the way our forefathers mined it. Experience taught them where to look for coal, and they sank small shafts down to the seams worth exploiting. They did not go deep enough to encounter gas, so could work with candles. A primitive hoist, worked sometimes by a horse, would get men and coal in and out of the pit. The waste rubbish caused by the pit sinking was spread around the top of the shaft or the hole they had made. Here and there mounds of dirt – hills of dirt. Hill in Welsh is *bryn*. Dirt is *baw*, put these together and you get *Brynbaw* – Brymbo. We natives called it Brumbo, but the refined way (or the way you said it over the telephone) was Brimbo, which could reflect the *brin* sound of *bryn*. At home on our telephone, we often got calls meant for Bromborough, so the more refined pronunciation over the phone was worthwhile. (Our telephone number in Brymbo was 214, the Bromborough Hospital was also 214; and for a young man who was becoming increasingly aware of the attractiveness of a particular nurse in Bromborough hospital, this was a very encouraging coincidence.)

Bethel Chapel had a house for its resident minister and his family. It was called Bryn Dwyfon and stood on a rise in the ground over looking the hill down to Brymbo Station. A new minister had arrived in Bethel and of course courtesy and curiosity made a call necessary (he had two daughters, which was another attraction). Sitting in the garden with one of them, I noticed that the garden 'soil' seemed nothing but fine coal dust. I asked Dad if he knew why.

He knew alright. The site of the Manse was a small pit. He remembered as a small boy seeing the shallow pit, the pit sinking debris, and a horse 'whimsy' or hoist. The garden was the top of the old workings.

During the long 1921 strike, more and more out-of-work colliers decided to ply their trade to keep their home warm and also to supply the growing demand for coal from firms across the border in Lancashire and Cheshire. Men set to, on their own or with comrades, to satisfy the demand. Looking out from the back of the Old Vicarage we saw the beginnings of a mine alongside the steep path that climbed from the Queens Head Inn to Clayton Road and Bryn Sion Chapel. Others found coal on the rising ground below the Drill Hall on Clayton Road; their coal was brought to the roadside above Brymbo Station signal box. Soon lorries, steam, oil and petrol from afar came to load up this coal for cross border industry. All this made me curious about Brymbo as it was before the industrial revolution. After all, I lived in a house that started as an old Welsh long-house.

I asked an old man, once a collier, if he could help me. He said: 'In Brymbo, the coal comes up with the sun and goes down with the sun.' I took this to mean that in a much older age, Brymbo's terrain had been folded by geological forces and then eroded, so that with some of the over-burden eroded the seams of coal were visible as outcrops, running from east to west.

On going through an old scrap book of my father's and grandfather's contributions to the *Wrexham Advertiser*, I came across a story about the *Great Western Railway* company's search for a water supply for the Brymbo Locomotives. They found a useful looking pool at the bottom of Pleasant Lane, on railway property, and decided to enlarge it. They found a healthy outcrop and the citizens of Brymbo helped themselves with buckets, wheel-barrows, donkeys and carts. Having read about the huge deposits of lignite, in German 'soft coal', I was curious about the product of the levels and went to see it and was not impressed with this coal. It seemed friable and lacked the hard shine of deep mined coal.

My father, worried about the effects this haphazard mining might have on water-mains, decided to investigate in the evenings, and to my joy invited us along. We saw some strange sights. Where the Mold-Coed Talon line turned from the fields below Church, by Pen-y-coed bridge on the Chester-Corwen Road, a steep little path led to a site we called Sadlers Woods. We found men busy in the dusk. They dug into the face of the slope and found coal in 'levels' workings. We called them levels to distinguish them from pits or shafts. There were fires, and paraffin flares, candles and Hurricane lamps bobbing about against the darker hillside – it made me think of the Klondyke.

Coal was being loaded into big wooden boxes, some home-made of rough sawn timber; others were stencilled with household product names. Ropes were tied to the boxes and they were being dragged out and their contents dumped nearby. Lorries loaded up here. There was an attitude of co-operation and self-help here that was invigorating. These men were keeping their homes warm.

We made more excursions – mainly in Broughton, where one company of colliers had commandeered their mothers' mangle and made a workmanlike haulage out of their pit. I was invited to drop down into one pit, near Pentre Broughton School, and did so with just a suspicion of dread. Another one which I seem to remember was near the old Brake tunnel which allowed wagons of an early railway to Brymbo, after being hauled up the 'brake' (an inclined railway), go via the tunnel which emerged (and was still visible in my younger days) near Brymbo Station. The name of Brake Chapel, a Wesleyan Chapel near the entrance to the tunnel, remembers it.

Incidentally my Father was a pupil teacher at Pentre Broughton School and the very stern headmaster was Jacob Astle. The school log book recalls that when the daughter of a prominent coal owner William Lowe of Tan-y-fron was about to be married the pupils of the school were given a special party with lots of lemonade. Quite a crisis arose when it was found out that one boy and some girls had been in the tunnel gloom quite late in the evening of the day of the nuptial celebrations.They had been reported to the school managers and warned about such conduct. In my teens the entrance to the tunnel to the Brake Chapel was visible. But now no more – did the wedding celebrations escapade hasten its cover-up?

Incidentally this same William Lowe published in 1865 a complete engineering plan for the Channel Tunnel, costed out fully in stirling, and designed to be ventilated, as were contemporary coal pits, by huge fires in the 'upcast' shaft. I wonder how that would go down today?

A popular walk from Brymbo was up over the fields towards Offa's Dyke. A pleasant red-ash path led up to a stile below which the land dropped steeply to a hollow. Menacing the whole area, crowning a small hill, was a large brick and stone circular wall guarding an old coal shaft. These things gave me the creeps. How deep were they? What was it like down there? An exploratory large stone thrown down brought a hideous hollow splash. My blood ran cold when I contemplated what might lie below.

Then came the magic formula I discovered in Physics (or was it mechanics?) in Grove Park School. It went (I hope I've got it right) $F = UT + \frac{1}{2}$ ft squared. From this if you timed accurately how long it took for the stone to hit the water at the bottom of that ghoulish shaft after release at the horrible wall above it you could work out the depth of the shaft. I can't remember now what it worked out at but it was very disturbing!

Apart from wondering what Offa might have thought if he'd known he was building his Dyke on a very big coalfield (he must have found an outcrop or two?), I wondered how many shafts had been opened here since the Industrial Revolution started.

Since meditating on my *Old Brymbo*, I asked the Welsh National Library at Aberystwyth for help. I had Ordinance Survey Maps 1900 and 1899 which astonished me. Brymbo – its whole area – is pitted with hundreds of old shafts. These, in turn, called into being scores of tramways to get their products to selling points. All, now, like the pits that spawned them, are just marks on an old map.

Chapter 10

Brymbo Steelworks

For most of my life, Brymbo could not be imagined without its steelworks. As is well known, John Wilkinson started it all in 1796; there was ironstone near the site and coal was to be had in plenty. After some vicissitude and with lines being laid down by the Brymbo Mineral Railway, gradually considerable trackage was built up and an involvement in the line from Wrexham which reached Brymbo by an easterly route. This included a roped incline (in parlance of the day a 'Brake') which came up to Broughton, near where the Brake Wesleyan Chapel now stands, and reached Brymbo Station site by a short tunnel.

With increasing demand for steel and open-hearth processing, Brymbo works became the Brymbo Steel Company Limited and produced its first steel in January 1885. During the great depression of the '30s', I was present with my camera when the new blast furnace was 'blown up' to great rejoicing in 1934.

Hugh and I were at once attracted to the steelworks engines and soon knew them all as much by sound as sight. One of the first we got to know was an 0-6-0 saddle tank with inside cylinders; for some reason the clean lines of the inside cylindered engine appealed to us both. *Bobs* was built by Hunslet in 1888; I think she was named after one of the British generals who put all those red marks on the maps of the world.

Snowdon was even earlier in my memory: it was a smaller 0-4-0 saddle tank with outside cylinders. It was the name of our highest mountain that took our fancy; as an engine it was a thing almost not worth knowing amidst the goodies otherwise about.

Basic was another oddity – an 0-4-0 crane tank engine which wore its crane jib along the tank top and looked like a hunch-back to us: we liked engines to be engines and look the part! *Gwynedd* was an 0-6-0 saddle tank whom we liked because of its name and ruggedness: I saw it last in the late 50's so it lasted well.

With *Anzac* (we took this as a compliment to the overseas Empire allies Australia and New Zealand), there came newer and, it seemed to us, larger engines. Anzac was followed by *Arenig* later in 1917. These were the engines we knew and liked; in our time diesels had not appeared, for which we are thankful!

Come with me from 16 Railway Road as I recall it as a child: we turn right and wait for the wicket gate on the big 4-track crossing to be unlocked from the signal box; maybe a train is due and the man in the box finds it safe to let us cross. We go over with a glance left at the rails leading up to the works. We climb past the end of Harward Road to the Cross, passing on our right St John's Welsh Church where our grandparents are buried. A left turn takes us into the High Street: passing more chapels and the Brymbo Co-operative Stores – grocery, gents and ladies outfitters, and a bakery; above us on our right looms the mass of Top yr Ochr; ahead on the right the long low whitewashed Blast Row (if you were ever in Ebbw Vale in its hey-day, you must have noticed a remarkably similar row of workmen's houses just as depressing!)

Now left to approach the steelworks; at the top of the hill, a biggish stone building with all the usual signs of a busy forge where Brymbo's horses were brought to be shod. Here too we brought out iron hoops which had suffered in some schoolboy over-zealousness and needed heating in the forge and welding into a hoop again. It was a magic place for a small boy, but a very busy one, and big horses with their flashing hooves and the thick blue choking smell of the hot shoes sizzling as the smith fitted them on the knifed-out horny hooves were a bit unnerving!

We turn right below a small hot-pool which steamed on cold days and beside which a narrow lane leads to the Mount Hotel and a few dwellings – including a chip-shop with a lift to take hot plates to a dining room above. I had seen the young bloods of Brymbo there, sitting on tall stools and eating tripe.

But we are approaching the steelworks and an ungated crossing of a railway leading from the very heart of the steelworks and its blast furnace complex. A loud engine whistle and a shout from a shunter and 'ladles' – heavy waggons with spouts dripping recently molten slag trundle heavily past on the way to the left bank of the steelworks where later an engine will couple on to the chains, haul back and tip the ladles to send their contents crashing down the bank. Sometimes, if they had cooled enough, the slag would come out like a reluctant poached egg and slither soggily down; if it were 'younger', it would break up as it left the ladle and flood the place with a gory light.

We pass the level crossing and emerge into a more open space with part of the electricity generating station – known to us as the 'power-house' – on the left and more railway tracks ahead. They come from the right and molten metal come past to go into the cavernous hell of the furnaces building where metal boils like toffee in open hearth furnaces and, with sweat rags on their faces against the heat, men peer through blue spectacles over a shielding hand. A hooter sounds and a man on a gantry overhead pilots a long groping rusty grab which carries its charge of rusty scrap iron into the very flaming heart of the furnaces; steel shutters clang back and the work goes on.

Later more hell-like action as molten steel is tipped from ladles into moulds and left to cool as ingots.

Later, still red hot, they go to the rolling mill where they are guided by impervious steel arms into the correct 'roll' where the now red plastic steel is squeezed and pressed like pastry into the size and shape the customers want.

I have mentioned these rolls before – they kept us company during the night and we got to know just which roll and which shears made the music which was so dreadfully missed in the big shut-down from 1931 to 1934. In those days of the Great Depression when our busy, noisy brightly-lit neighbour fell silent; when jazz bands flourished in Brymbo and out-of-work men and their wives and friends opened craft centres where men could get leather and nails and lasts to mend their children's shoes, and mothers did their bit for their clothes.

When I was working in Cardiff and Brymbo Steelworks shut down I came home on holiday and so missed the company of engine whistles and the many noises of the night in the busy steelworks that I just couldn't sleep. My father missed the noise of what he called 'the babcock' – a big steam boiler that every now and then whistled for water. But the unnerving thing was the black darkness that lay like a cloud over what had been a busy and bustling neighbour. I didn't enjoy that holiday at all!

There were many night noises, naturally. Somewhere in the works the 'shears', both 'top' and 'bottom' made jangling steel noises. Small engines puffed and hooted; steam cranes, which could be driven around like clockwork cats, jib a-dangle, growled through their gears; a rake of heavy tippers, just loaded with molten slag, clanked their weight over adequate, but not refined, level crossings over other internal rail trackways; a spate of shunting, engine whistles and hoarse commands meant a locomotive was set to haul at a long chain that went through the tipping gear of the ladles; and the bump of falling, glowing stone would end as the load tumbled down the steelworks bank and broke open, flooding the countryside with glowing yellow light.

But, back to the open space where the rails led out of the hot metal area past the fitting shop, where a road ran down on the left narrowly to the Lodge with the diminishing bulk of the Steelworks Bank on the left and the site of the Brymbo Station of the *Great Central* (Cheshire Lines and LNER Railway) on the right. We had its station-master living next door to us in our Bryn Awel house but I have no memory of passenger trains. The picture I have of its station came from my father, and as far as I know is unique.

Just where the Lodge road turned down, two paths led upward. One climbed steeply past the laboratory of the Steelworks and led to Brymbo Hall and Brymbo Cricket ground. Here the 1914-18 volunteers were taught to shoot on indoor ranges – and I spent a lot of time with my father and brother here. Here too were the 'Top' Offices, and the steelworks railways swept round past the long closed Blast Pit and on up to the Wonder Bank and the Works Engine Sheds.

It ran up for a few hundred yards by the side of the road which continued to Top Brymbo Pool, then reversed by quite a steep climb which, when one of the more robust locomotives was on the train with a reasonably worthwhile load, made for quite dramatic engine noises. The line then fanned out into a shunting yard which was typically haphazard in terms of track excellence: how there were not far more derailments I cannot imagine.

And talking about derailments, one particular one stands out in my memory: the steam cranes in use were locomotives in the sense that the drivers, by selecting suitable gearing, could turn their cylinder power to the wheels. But they were not really practicable locomotives and – especially on some parts of the works tracks – not to be used without caution. As we came home from school on one particular day, we noticed unusual activity on the tracks leading up from Brymbo West crossing to the works; a crane on its side across the rails had only one reason: one of the crane drivers had ventured on to a difficult part of the track, lost control and turned over. There were worried men and hushed voices around Brymbo West crossing: I think the crane driver died from his injuries.

The only other dramatic mishap we heard as a loud bang; molten slag from the steel furnace had been run off into a ladle which had water in it. It blew up like a bomb: there were casualties of course.

We left our walk around the works near the second level crossing where ladles full of molten iron crossed the road which led to the furnaces.

A right turn here took the tracks past shunting yards usually full of waggons of scrap metal. Higher up was an erection that looked like a poor attempt at a transporter bridge; just as raw boned. A large round, flat object was slung from the bridge by chains and trailed heavy rubber cables: it was in fact a large magnet which was sent squashing down into a waggon-load of scrap and came out of the waggon trailing bits and pieces rather aimlessly. But several waggon-loads of scrap lying ready for the furnaces testified to its eventual usefulness. In this area my Sunday school teacher, who knew of my interest in Meccano, found some recognisable but too badly distorted bits of Meccano parts, which sent me searching there on week-ends with total no-success.

I said that the railway leading to the Wonder Bank ran along a road that went to Top Brymbo Pool. This was a large stretch of water fed at the top end by a Brymbo Water Company's Kennedy meter.

It was a positive meter, not an inferential one. In other words, as I understand it, it measured the flow through it accurately. It was a big instrument and inside it had a large hammer-like lever which rocked backwards and forwards against large rubber blocks. It made a loud bang as it did so and was reputed to scare courting couples and engendered a belief in ghostly evening visitors, as well as flesh and blood ones.

It was a popular evening and after-chapel stroll; my first memory of it – and my only real memory of my grandfather – was when he threw an allegedly smelly Tango, our family Welsh Terrier, into it to the tearful wrath of both Hugh and me.

John Wilkinson, the Ironmaster mined lead ore in Minera in the 1790's, the ore being brought down to the 'Smelt' as the area was known in our time. Here he set up works to produce the lead. The fumes from this works were poisonous and to disperse them the Bottle Chimney was built. The fumes were carried to the chimney by 'tunnels', and inside the chimney galleries were built to recover the lead oxide.

The chimney was a landmark visible for many miles. It had a conical base with an orthodox chimney above. It was an eerie place at the best of times with quite a sharp updraft. Only one other place caused me as much uneasiness; Dad took us to see the 'Fan' which ventilated the Westminster (Moss) Colliery; it stood on a hilltop near Gwersyllt. After Dad had finished his talk with the men who ran the ventilation Hugh and I were both invited in to see the 'Fan'.

A large door opened into a nightmare of plucking searching winds in a long tunnel sloping down to some unimaginable horror in the distance: the sloping shaft was lined entirely with glazed white tiles. I was terrified; all I could think of was being down the long white oubliette: it was Edgar Allen Poe's worst thriller concept. Since Westminster Colliery closed down after the 1926 strike I must have at a very impressionable age. And I'd read a lot of Edgar Allen Poe's books.

The nearby Carbon Works, I was once told, was where carbon rods for early electric arc lamps were made. I do know that a large and heavy table that came from the works ended up in our playroom and was used on one well-remembered wet day as a 'munition factory' (this was 1915) in which the chief process was smashing marbles on its stout top. No need to say why we remembered the day? Not so much later Hugh and I had to have out tonsils and adenoids removed. Dr Geoffrey Williams of Wrexham and his father did the job. I came round half-way through, convinced I was a well and people were sticking ladders down me. This was on the same table; as I was being taken off to bed I noticed a white bucket with blood splashes under the table. Somebody – it was a female voice, and the only one I think I recognised was my mother's household help – said unfeelingly 'Blackpuddings for Supper!'

There was nowhere in Brymbo where you could swim. Top Brymbo Pool was used now and again: I remember a day when three boys were drowned there. Brymbo and Broughton were in mourning.

There was another so-called 'Hot Pool' below Brymbo Pool, but it was smelly and uninviting.

Chapter 11

Bethel Chapel

When I was a boy ministers of religion were important people: if they were powerful preachers they were that much more highly prized. A carefully worked out system – 'The Plan' – arranged their preaching commitments for months ahead. There were also more lowly – but much liked – lay assistants who could fill a pulpit in emergencies. Wesleyans called them *pregethwyr cynorthwyol* – assistants in the pulpit. Their ability was carefully assessed and they were trained to go on to more demanding roles in Wesleyan Methodism.

Whenever a 'planned' preacher failed to keep his *cyhoeddiad*, his schedule, a 'prayer meeting' was held when men – or women – who had proved their ability were called upon. Usually this meant a shortened service with no sermon. The people who took part welcomed the chance to show their ability to maintain a service and to entertain a congregation. To us youngsters, the second duty was the spice of the arrangement. Each of the volunteers made the most of their opportunity and we got to know their more entertaining pulpit mannerisms. Some perplexed us: a greengrocer of otherwise mild manner astonished – and at first alarmed – us by sobbing wildly as his message to his maker progressed. The first time Hugh and I heard him we shrank down in our seats in the gallery. Dad was too interested to notice: Mother signalled us to be calm, and as soon as she was able, told us that this was just the man's usual way of getting his message across and we were not to worry. Others we liked for other reasons. A mild and likeable man we heard talked of as '*Bob dau grys*' ('Bob two shirts'). 'Why two shirts?' we asked my father. His reply was not quite convincing – that one time he had only one shirt, 'Did he have to go to bed when his mother washed it?' asked Hugh. 'When did he get enough money from his mother for another shirt?' I asked. Were they very poor? Questions, questions . . .

Between both our parents we found that he sweated so much on the steel furnaces that he had to have two shirts to go to work.

In the hard and driving times in which we lived, the pulpit was for many young – and not so young – men a chance to make progress. My uncle, Richard Jones-Williams, for example, almost always had around him a class of earnest young men desperately anxious to escape from the coal pit or the steelworks by training for the ministry. They were the men the nonconformists church looked to for their future leaders.

Wesleyanism was a pillar of my Father's life and of his father's and mother's before him. Wesleyan ministers served three years in each chapel and circuit to which they were allotted. Each minister had a manse for his family and it included all that they and their families needed except personal things like bed linen.

When my grandmother's obituary was written much praise was given for her stewardship in looking after the comfort and happiness of young ministers and their families settling in to their new homes. My father's sister married a handsome Barmouth minister and his daughter had told me of the great trauma of the forced uprooting. What she remembers most was the prickly horsehair upholstery of John Wesley's chairs! To us boys the triennial change over of the Manse family was eagerly anticipated: in Bethel the Bryn Dwyfon (Manse) family sat in their preordained seat under the gallery on the left of the chapel.

Brymbo in my young days was very much a church and chapel going community. After sitting with my mother quietly in my bedroom on Sunday nights (Dad having gone of course to this mystery place, chapel, to which all the men and women in their best clothes were trooping, while my mother watched [it was a summer evening] behind the net curtains) I began to have a powerful curiosity to know what it was all about.

Bethel Welsh Wesleyan Chapel had been opened in 1895. It was strategically sited opposite Brymbo Station so that it served congregations in Brymbo, Lodge, Broughton and New Broughton, all of whom found it an easy walk.

Bethel was typical of its times. I know that in the early days when I was first allowed to go to Sunday night meetings I have seen it, from our seat in the Gallery level with the Pulpit (my mother's hearing was slightly defective) crowded: every seat full.

Bethel was also typical of its class. It held 500 and the main meeting place was on the first floor; as one went in by the main door, stairs led right and left to large gallery accommodation, two doors faced the congregation, that on the right was a cupboard and that on the left led to the vestry, really a room for the occupier of the pulpit to prepare himself for his ordeal. The room included all the amenities, including a brush and comb. Stairs led down to a large school room full of varnished benches backs of which swung to allow classes to be easily arranged, and at the far end, a stage. This school room covered the ground plan of the chapel. At the other end on the left was another small room, and the stairs that led up to the vestry.

The pulpit was placed with a commanding view of the congregation. Elegant steps led up on both sides of it, but the whole noble sweep of the pulpit end lacked one essential – a pipe organ. In front of the pulpit area and enclosing it was a very powerful element in the Chapel life – *Y Sêt Fawr*, the 'grand seat'. This was occupied by the chapel's rulers, the deacons, who seemed to hold the power of life or death over the congregation. Those children who had learned a verse had to go and stand at the high (to us) back of the *Sêt Fawr* to recite to the congregation. This meant that (fortunately) we could not see our parents' worried faces, but we faced the minister who has now descended from the pulpit to hear our verses, while the deacons twisted on their seats to give us fair play.

For the youngest of us it was customary to lessen the trauma by choosing a three word verse – *'Duw cariad yw'*, ('God is love'), or *'Yr Iesu a Wylodd'* ('Jesus wept'). As we grew older the task grew harder and our stage fright worse. Since the reciters on a normal Sunday evening service would fill the space behind the *Sêt Fawr* each carried a formidable burden; before us ranks of old Deacons in their stiff Sunday best, and confronting us the minister of the day.

Towards the front of the chapel was an harmonium – quite a good one, but without the grand array of pipes that any good chapel demanded. From the harmonium's right hand side a long handle emerged: I early learned to hate it. Whoever supplied the wind for the organ was the slave of a nasty black bobbin that had to be kept at the top of its travel. It always sank lower and lower until I thought I could never find enough energy to pump up to its due place again!

Although I went there unwillingly as a small boy I am conscious of the way Bethel shaped my young ideas and built into my life some standards that no longer seem to apply. My father was a Sunday School Teacher and a chapel member of great probity. Once in some hard times in the days of the Depression, someone – a business acquaintance – sent him a turkey as a Christmas present. He sent it back with a polite note of refusal, while we children whose great treat had been chicken and whose comic papers were full of Christmas crackers and similar bung-ho stood around with long faces.

He told us, quite simply, then why he had to refuse such a

compromising gift. We believed him, with regret for a lost Christmas dinner – roast turkey was a rich rarity in our lives of leg of lamb. But the lesson was learned.

In our days there were no Youth Clubs or any places where boys and girls busily growing up could acquire – I was about to say the social graces – but that's an overshoot! What I mean is a chance to mix with girls or boys and enjoy the first preliminaries that led to closer acquaintances and so, in the fullness of time, to marriage and one's own family life.

As a chapel member, although a lively advocate of the social side for enjoyment among other chapel youngsters I could never have imagined organising a dance! A tea party of the least adventurous kind – yes. Whist drive? Utterly impossible! We had debating society meetings where I can remember some very radical speeches from older Sunday school teachers; it was here I first heard the tenets of Communism, even.

One important annual event in Bethel was the Good Friday Concert: much anticipated, however much I rebelled against the way it was organised. Our Young People's Society worked all through the winter season to generate funds. But when the call for money for the concert came, all our hard-earned balance was swallowed up in an event which itself made only a meagre profit. Perhaps I had too narrow a view of the whole idea, for it was a memorable musical event. It also brought much kudos to the organisers and to our chapel.

I should remind you of the almost suffocating effect of the non-conformist idea of the Sabbath observation, and of course Good Friday was very much given the respect that Sunday had.

Good Friday was a day of no amusement for us children. We were allowed no recreation as we know it now. Best Sunday clothes and no activity to disturb a godly silence. (It still offends my feelings of propriety when I hear children playing noisy games on Sunday!)

Once the Brymbo Cinema was established the same strict rules applied. No shows on Good Friday! Then a whisper of great change with the advent of silent films with a religious theme. We agonised about the portrayal of Jesus – would an actor be allowed to play the part? If so – who? So the last bastion fell and Brymbo Picturehouse opened on Good Friday.

But Bethel's Good Friday Concert still was Bethel's great night. Scouts went out around North Wales seeking suitable talent; a Buckley musician was the Go Between, the Impresario.

Dad was pressed one night to join the deputation to Buckley. We saw him off as though he was about to visit Buckingham Palace. He went with the other ambassadors in somebody's Ford Model T. Somewhere on the way the engine died. Out of petrol?

The Model T tank was under the front seat cushion. Sufficient of the passengers got out to allow the petrol filler cap to be removed and the tank plumbed: no stick seemed deep enough, so some struck a match. My father had to convince Mama that the dirt on his face and his general non-ambassadorial outer wear was caused by a panic 'abandon Ship' and no one was hurt – just aware that petrol and matches didn't go well together.

In Bethel, ladies of the congregation dusted and polished and urged the men – and boys! – to get the stage up. This meant covering the *Sêt Fawr* with a decking fit to bear the weightiest artist (artiste?) and solid enough for the most nervous soprano.

Part of the magic of the night to us uncultured youngsters was the splendid concert attire of women and men singers. The men in stiff white shirts, collars, and black ties. But – the ladies! Apart from Walter Roberts' Pantomime in Wrexham we had only seen stage shows to rival this in silent film in the Brymbo pictures!

To a boy we envied the immaculate compere – usually the impresario who had brought them all together, who with negligent but smiling aplomb took the hand of the retiring goddess as she left the stage and saw her safety to ground level. That seemed to one small boy at least the most desirable job in the world!

All seats had of course been filled. In addition perspiring younger men had brought forms from the school room to seat even more concert goers. On a cold night – it was March as a rule – the combined exhalations of the paraffin lamps and the congregation ran down in streams of condensation from the painted walls. More than one young blood who had taken his lady guest to a secluded seat in the windows around the gallery recesses found pools of condensation accumulating in uncomfortable places beneath him.

Myself, I didn't much care for the more massive sopranos: what I loved were the items usually given as encores – and there was a babel of demand until we got them – of the light touch – 'Madame, will you walk and talk with me' and 'Will you give me the keys of your heart' – the simple things that I, years later at Ebbw Vale National Eisteddfod heard that great artist Paul Robeson sing with a simplicity that moved me to tears.

I don't ever remember any open opposition to the Good Friday Concert. In your young minds it was classed on a par with that other festival – Shrove Tuesday, which brought us Pancake Day.

71

Tom Edwards, by his musical ability, was one of the men who influenced Bethel more than most. He had left us to emigrate to Patagonia in the early years of the century but then left his adopted country to come back to Wales when the 1914-18 war broke out. He brought with him a wife who could speak only Spanish and Welsh and three children – Maelor, a son of the first marriage, and three daughters – Camwy, Eira Sian and Carys.

They were, as a family, a reminder of the great surge of desire in all parts of Wales to seek out new lives where the Welsh way of life would be free of religious intolerance and landlords who demanded that their tenants should vote according to the landlord's politics and not the tenants' convictions. The story started in Llanbrynmair with 'S.R.' and like minded people and found its followers in many parts of Wales; in the quarries, the iron works, the mines, and the workers from the farms and the countryside. You will know how early would-be settlers landed on an inhospitable coast in far off South America and lived in caves along the shore until they ventured inland and founded a fragile existence.

*　*　*

Anticipation burned in us as we saw from my Mother's shopping list that the extras such as eggs and – joy! – lemons were included. Came the day – it always seems to have been a Wednesday, not Tuesday to me. We rushed home from school to the expected cosy kitchen, tidy and prepared for good things once the necessary chores of the day had been done: and all was ready for the feast.

The big black frying pan was gleamingly ready. From the white scrubbed kitchen table rows of eggs and lemons had gone but a large white bowl with a snowy white cloth over it promised many pleasures.

Dad came in from his office: expectation heightened. The polished frying pan came down from the *pentan* and my mother rolled her sleeves up and we, hushed but excited waited as my mother put the pan to warm, filled a cup with the bowl's white creamy liquid. A hiss as she poured it into the pan, a long sigh as we watched it spread and slowly stiffen. A quick juggle of the pan allowed the unset portion to flow around the couple of lazy bubbles and the Shrove Tuesday treat showed itself to our delighted eyes: there was no tossing so rich and rare a phenomenon, naturally: a large bowl just the diameter of the pancake's promise was filled with boiling water and put on the table after many warnings of the most dire consequences to further pancake adventures if the hot bowl was overturned by our over-eagerness . . . one pancake safely in place on its plate on the steaming bowl, a drift of castor sugar from a shaker, a squeeze of lemon, a careful cut to make the right size segments . . . and a withdrawal of the encircling children to let the show continue . . . as the plate filled with golden promise and as sugar and lemon juice went on our suffering was almost unbearable.

I'm sure that you who have been through similar family pancake sessions will know what happens next. We had a saying that so-and-so's eyes were bigger than his stomach . . . and as the segments vanished so did our appetites. But what a treat to remember!

Chapter 12

Characters

Samuel Charles Hughes – whenever Hugh and I heard my mother and father converse in Welsh using '22 High Street' we knew that we should listen. For this is where one of the best known of Brymbo figures lived with his sister Ellen Esther – otherwise known as 'Auntie Etta'.

Samuel Charles Hughes was a cousin of my father's, a public figure of some importance. He had an office with a front door on High Street which in time became the then equivalent of a Labour Exchange. Here I, in my first weeks in Wrexham County School, was found a part-time job by my father. I have a vivid memory of a Samuel Shallcross who walked all the way from beyond Ffrith to 'sign on', this he did with a huge black pencil cross, and I felt very sorry for him. The only thing I remember was a voice-pipe down which Uncle Samuel used to blow when he wanted to speak with his sister; it was an office worthy of Dickens.

In some family crisis Hugh and I infrequently enjoyed the overwhelming luxury of Auntie Etta's feather bed: my mother's choice was blankets without sheets for the winter.

We both fell in love with the downstairs old fashioned WC housed in a small room decorated with what seemed a century of cartoons and coloured pictures from the best Liberal publications. They were a perpetual source of joy to us young readers. During the 1921 coal strike Auntie Etta ran a series of soup kitchens for strikers' children. My mother had been called urgently to South Wales where her uncle was seriously ill. Every night Dad, Hugh and I went to Auntie Etta's snug kitchen where she later arrived with a very large can full of hot pea soup. She also bought with her a copy of the *Daily Sketch*, where we first saw cartoon comic strips of 'Mutt & Jeff' and 'Mrs Jiggs', 'Uncle Samuel' as we knew him achieved fame in our eyes at least by being taken to America by a temperance organisation called the 'Good Templars'.

Our next door neighbour to the Old Vicarage was the Sambrook family – Mr Sambrook in his immaculate G.W.R. uniform was the signalman at Brymbo Middle signal box. Later he was promoted – Station Inspector Wrexham.

No local carnival was complete without the jockey-like figure of John Sammy Joseph, who enlivened Haward Road with his horsey get up.

Bethel Chapel morning service started at 10.00. On our way from the Old Vicarage we went down what we called 'Dick-y-Paraffin' Hill, as we did so – in the distance – we saw the Headmaster of Pentre Broughton School – Dai Rees, charging past Lloydie Row on his way past the *Queens Head* and the *Prince of Wales* to the Cross Chapel where he was the precentor.

Another faithful commuter from halfway down Pisgah Hill, twice on Sundays to the same Chapel was William Roberts, who worked in the offices of the Brymbo Water Company and later became the Manager.

Where Dick-y-Paraffin Hill came down to the Tai Road one family apparently occupied a row of cottages. On my way to chapel one Sunday morning I noticed a magnet on the wall in front of Joe Green's house and stopped to look at it. Joe 'Green' (his real name was Davies) came out and we made an instant friendship based on love of and interest in the motor car. I had known for some time the handsome woman who passed the Old Vicarage carrying on her head a loaded basket. This was not unusual in Brymbo, but this woman's grace of carriage and erect figure was outstanding. She was Joe's mother and the family matriarch. Joe and his brother used to go weekly to St John's Market in Liverpool to buy produce for their vegetable round in Brymbo, and I enjoyed many an early morning run in their light lorry to Liverpool. The lorry had been converted from a pre-war Belsize Bradshaw coupe, and was a fascinating period piece to drive.

My father's elder brother Thomas Owen Charles emigrated to America in the closing years of the old century and settled in Scranton. He was a newspaper man and became editor and then proprietor of *Y Drych* – The Mirror, a Welsh language newspaper. In a special corner of Dad's part of the Old Vicarage was a simple chair – a light folding wooden frame with a piece of carpet for a seat. This was referred as 'Nain Charles' steamer chair'. She had made two voyages to America 'in steerage' to see Thomas Owen Charles and his family. His first wife – a Brymbo woman born in Coed-y-Felin – had died; he had married again and Nain Charles wanted to see how her son was doing. In fact he became a pillar of society in Scranton. He died of pneumonia in 1916 and had weakened his health working for the Welsh cause in a big exhibition which included a vast *eisteddfod*. In a letter just before he died he wrote of day-long wearisome journeys in unheated trains. In 1924, his widow and two daughters visited Wales, and did a round of the family in Brymbo, Caernarfon and London. Their accents were very 'Eastern Seaboard American' and Hugh and I had to explain to our distracted mother that 'burrer' meant butter and 'warrer' meant water, and so on. I am still puzzled how we could so efficiently translate their Americanisms. Talking pictures had not yet been invented. I now know that his daughters worked for an Eastern seaboard film producing company, and moved to Hollywood when the talkies came. We have since lost touch, regrettably, with our American cousins. Among other treasures time robbed me of were huge picture books – 'coffee table books' we'd call them today – of the enormous mile-long coal trains crawling up famous mountain ranges between coalfields and the industrial inlands. As I remember they were very well printed and immaculately produced. All this led to a great interest in transatlantic shipping; I remember my father's horror at the *Titanic* disaster, and much more clearly the shock of the torpedoing of the beautiful turbine driven Blue Riband holder *Lusitania* off the Old Head of Kinsale in Ireland.

* * *

As small boys we were given many brochures published by White Star, and Cunard and the Canadian Railways which fostered the emigration trend as America and Canada sought new citizens from Europe. Perhaps my grandfather had some sort of side-line as a travel agent, because we always had, spread out on the living room floor, many colourful brochures advertising the attractions of Canada and the prairie states – so that Manitoba and Saskatchewan and the Great Lakes became part of our everyday playtime. The great liners of these times became household words to us – so you can imagine what a disaster the Titanic was.

Indeed my most abiding memory of breakfasts during the worst years of the U boat offensive of the 1914-18 war was of my father's gloom as he disappeared to his office in the front of the house trailing clouds of smoke over his shoulder and lamenting the *Lusitania* or the *Britannic*.

* * *

Nurse Elizabeth – 'Lily' – Reade had been brought up by her grandparents in Caernarfonshire. Her father, a house painter, had left Pwllheli and worked in Lymm, in Cheshire.

Ill-health had made her parents send her into her grandparents' care. Her grandmother had become very deaf, and when, in better times her parents wanted Lily back, the grandmother totally refused to part with the little girl who was now 'her ears and her eyes'. Her grandfather, who was a night station master at Bangor LNWR Station had been offered a retirement job as station master at Glan Conwy but was allergic to sea-weed smells and was offered Treborth Station on the Bangor-Afon Wen Branch.

After the deaths of her grandparents my mother was taken into the care of an aunt, one of their daughters, who had married a young doctor who practised first in Llangollen and then had jointed his brother in a medical practise in the booming South Wales coalfield and had surgeries in Miskin, Mountain Ash and Abercynon. Dr Hugh Davies Jones was an original: he had two sons and four daughters, with my mother as a big sister to his family. The family name was Davies-Jones, which he disliked. 'Too many Davieses and Joneses in Wales,' he said, and changed the family name to Pierce – but only for his two boys and one daughter, Gwen. (When I later on worked on Cardiff, Aberdare and Merthyr newspapers and had friends in Mountain Ash the double nomenclature became hard to explain!)

The doctor was ahead of his times in insisting that all his daughters – my mother included – followed careers of their own. The two elder girls went to Cardiff to become domestic science teachers. Dilys trained as a business secretary: the youngest, Dorothy, a very good golfer, was the first girl to pass the RAC driving test in Cardiff, I was told: she went on to become her father's chauffeur when the first World War took his men drivers. How that girl handled the family Austin 12 on the precipitous hills of urban hilly Glamorgan was an inspiration. In some streets there the front doorstep of one house in the endless terraces was level with the windowsills of the next. My mother followed the Doctor's plans for his family and went to Chester Royal Infirmary to be trained for nursing. She then went on to do her 'District' training in Canton, Cardiff. She was there for one of the last typhoid epidemic scares in this country and was told to clear all the bedding of a suspect house while the patient's husband was at work. She and her nurse-trainer threw the bedding out of a bedroom window and scored a direct hit as he came home for his tea!

From time to time my mother's services as a nurse were called for in urgent cases, or when the Queen's Nurse was busy or on leave. You can imagine my surprise when I came home from school to find my mother absent – 'nursing Mr Peter Williams, ill with pneumonia'. But this was not the clogger, but a man of considerable importance: the head of Brymbo Steelworks. I think he had helped the Russians to modernise their steel production: I do know that Mama told me that he was learning and reading Greek in his sick bed. His son, Christmas Price Williams – 'C.P.' to us – became the last Liberal member for the old East Denbighshire seat. His wife was a patron of Dramatic art, and I was busy on one of her plays – *When Did You Last See Your Father*, a civil war incident when I received a telegram from Denbighshire Education Department to tell me that I had been awarded a scholarship which eventually took me to Kings College, London. I always travelled to London at the beginning of term on the *Zulu* – ex Wrexham 12.42, Birmingham 2.44, Paddington 5.29. This was a crack midday train with dining car service. 'C.P.' would look along the train at Wrexham and once or twice invited me to have lunch with him – 7 shillings.

Chapter 13

Coal Picking

One of my photographs, taken in the bad, bad old days in the thirties, came almost by accident. I had made a few bob taking some pictures for the *Wrexham Leader* and had to go to put some *Farmers Weekly* urgent pictures off to London (before the days of *Red Star* railway deliveries) so I took them to Chester to be trained to London. I called in Will R. Rose's photographic shop in the Rows and saw on offer out-of-date film packs at very bargain rates. They fitted the Anschutz plate press camera I was using and I set off for home thinking that if a picture presented itself I would be justified in trying an exposure. Coming back through Southsea, I thought of coal pickers working on waste coal tips from Plas Power Colliery. I found the tip and many men at work. They had suffered long hardship from the 30s depression and they wore not clothes but any covering that dirty job of coal picking on a bank burning under their feet might need. They pushed skeletons of old bicycles with an old sack of picked coal draped over where the chain wheel once had been. They had old bottles full of cold tea and bread and margarine wrapped up in old newspapers. Living at its most basic and cheerless.

I found out the reason why more pickers than usual were at work. Plas Power had received an order for a few waggonloads of coal urgently needed for Liverpool. Runners were sent out to get enough miners to come in to the pit. The runners sent the word that there'd be a little difficulty in filling the order without a little unavoidable waste which of course would be disposed of as usual on to the tip. A little joy for the pickers – and they needed it. Miners still at work – and they were all too few usually – left the cage on coming on the bank with a couple of log ends under their arms. Pit props, you understand, then had to be tailored to meet the needs of safety underground.

By the time I reached home, there were another three or four exposures left on the film pack. The midday goods train to Brymbo from

Coed Talon was due, so I climbed to the top of the boundary wall overlooking the railway and got a Webb 0-6-2 coal tank just coming over the crossing.

Years later, when *Y Cymro*, the newspaper I worked for, sent me on a story across the border I usually contrived to come down towards Wrexham via Coed-poeth and Brymbo – just for old time's sake. I stopped the car on the bridge outside the Old Vicarage and saw to my delight a long train coming over the Prince of Wales Crossing. But it had two *Great Western* – B.R. in fact of course – locomotives on it. All the time I had lived in Brymbo I had never – but never – seen a GWR engine on this line. Looking around we saw the reason why – the train had been lifting the permanent way lower down the branch: it was Beeching time, and I knew with a sinking heart that never again would I see rail traffic on the Mold to Brymbo branch of the former *LNWR*.

* * *

After my mother married my father, she left for a more important job but was asked to help from time to time when the second nurse was ill or on leave.

Often, in later years, this coincided with school holidays and I went with her if she needed company. In this way I got to know some interesting people. One was the Steelworks' chemist, a victim of advanced rheumatic fever which had left him almost immobile. My mother told me about him and how she had been inspired by something in the nursing magazines about the effect of heat in such cases.

Brymbo Steelworks had a powerhouse which fascinated me, with its advanced machinery for generating the large amount of current the steel processes needed. It was possible to go past the powerhouse and the men working with electrical equipment and having perforce, for safety reasons, always to stand on heavy rubber matting.

Impressed, but not more than by the motive power which drove the generators. I had expected soft purring turbines such as the main engines of the much mourned Lusitania and the thankfully remaining Mauritania, with their Parsons equipment which gave them speeds we reckoned to be as much as 35 land miles an hour and earned the Blue Riband of the Atlantic for the fastest crossing to America.

When I ventured past the 'powerhouse', I was much put out to find noisy gas engines fed on (I think) blast furnace gases which created a noisy rattle from what I perceived to be tappet valve gear. I understood later that this was the latest and best prime movers in the power production game.

My mother, aware of the uses of electricity in the steel works, decided to ask for help to ease Mr Barker's painful problems.

She persuaded some of the fitting-shop men to get an old cast-iron bath and festoon the inside of it with carbon filament electric lamps – an early type which produced as much heat as light.

It helped him very much and after his 'heat treatment', he found movement much freer and far less painful. I can only conclude after some painful attempts at amateur electricity myself that the skills and kindness of his workmen friends saved him from possible electrocution!

All this I heard from Mr Archer when I called with my mother. I had liked chemistry in school (and done well in it). I think his home was somewhere in what was Lodge: he had a small cosy house with a coal fire in an open grate which, as we used to find with some coal, tended to liquefy under heat and then shoot out puffs of gas. These became alight and soon the whole room would be suffused with falling trails of soot.

'I see you've got some very gassy coal,' I said, and was rather abashed when he told me in immaculate phrases the definitive description of the phenomenon. But he did it kindly, and I felt grateful.

Chapter 14

Luftwaffe hits Brymbo

This is Hugh's story of that night and its sequel.

'I was on firewatching duty with Thomas John Hughes, known to everyone as Twm, a mainlayer and maintenance man. It was the usual pattern, Jerry was over in strength, Liverpool was having a pasting and the anti-aircraft guns were banging away putting up a terrific barrage. Suddenly the bomb blasts seemed nearer, then without any warnings bombs fell in the village, down in the Green. We grabbed our tin helmets and dashed off down the road to where we thought the bombs had fallen, to see what damage had been done and to organise repair gangs if necessary. As we ran down the road we heard someone following us and later learned that it was Herbert Gott, who was in charge of the village A.R.P. We found that a bomb had fallen on the main road between the Queens Cross and the cinema, breaking a gas main and setting fire to the escaping gas.

'By this time a few village men had appeared and started throwing earth on the flames in a vain effort to put out the fire, since it was thought it would attract more bombs. After making sure that no damage had been done to our water mains we gave the A.R.P. a hand in checking the damage. The cinema had been badly damaged and a lock-up grocery shop blown off the road. We got in touch with the owners and Herbert Gott in the meantime had alerted the Gas Works about their broken main. The Gas Repair Gang were soon on the spot and when they found an undamaged end of the main stopped the leak and extinguished the fire.

'It was now about 3.00 and we all felt tired and sat down with our backs to Graingers' garden wall opposite to the Queens Head Inn. Jim Lloyd (Prince of Wales Cottage) said, 'It's a funny thing how this wall fell into the road towards where the bomb fell, you would expect it to fall into the garden away from the bomb.' This started a debate on the queer things that blast did, but Jim was not convinced and went through the remains of the wall to have a good look around in the rubble. Suddenly he shouted, 'Good God! Come and look at this.' 'This' was a hole about 2½ feet in diameter rimmed with a circular mound of dirt about 8 to 10 inches high. We all realised it was an unexploded bomb! The local policeman jumped on the bike and dashed off to the Lodge Police Station to report. In no time at all the Bomb Disposal unit came up and confirmed that it was an unexploded bomb. The officer took a man to show him where Herbert Gott lived while the rest of his team aided by the A.R.P. aroused the people in the adjoining houses. They, taking their 'emergency bundles' with them, went to the 'emergency centre' in the Brymbo Council School, where they lived until it was safe to return.

The bomb had fallen into very soft soil, and had gone deep. The Royal Engineers of the Bomb Disposal Unit had to be very careful and it took about ten days to get down to the bomb. It was found to be lying so awkwardly that it was deemed too dangerous to defuse it, so it had to be blown up. Mr Macdonald, the manager of the Queens Head felt it was his duty to keep an eye on the place whilst all this work was going on around it to get down to the bomb. He apparently did not know that the bomb was about to be detonated, and after the explosion, which wrecked the gable end of the building, everyone on the site were astounded to see him stagger out of the front door with blood streaming down his face.

My father and mother, in Cambrian House, heard the explosion and looking out of the kitchen window saw a policeman walking slowly back to view the damage. He stopped and took off his helmet, and Mother, very distressed, said, 'Oh dear, John – someone has been killed'. Then both realised that the policeman was mopping his brow!

During the same night bombs were dropped on the Brymbo Steelworks, at least one on the 'scraps', the area where scrap metal was stored, destroying waggons and smashing up the tracks. This blew pieces of scrap far and wide over the countryside and for many days afterwards tales were told of these bits being found in the most unlikely places – some being found over a mile from the site of the bomb blast.

'One of these was from Edward John Roberts, whose house on Clayton Road almost a mile away from the 'scraps' suffered when a fishplate broke the front room window cut through the back of the settee and smashed the wall into the kitchen. Fortunately no one was hurt. Mr Roberts was another of the Water Company staff involved – involuntarily – in the night's proceedings. Incidentally Hugh remembers seeing the tail fin of this bomb that damaged the Queens Cross, mounted on a plinth in the bar of the Black Lion Inn, very close to the scene of all the damage it caused.'

Chapter 15

The Gresford Disaster

I come now, at the last, to the Gresford Colliery disaster of September 1934 – to the explosion that killed 245 men. We are talking about small, village communities; one person acquainted with that generation of Gresford miners remembers that 'every night we would hear them pass the house in the dark, singing – usually Welsh hymns. They had walked several miles already and they still had two more miles to the pit; and then they would walk back through the underground passages to the seams. We would hear them sometimes on a still night hammering almost under the house. I used to like to hear them when I was curled up in bed as a small child. I always felt very near to them.'

Georgie Moulder was a man who befriended me greatly after I had left Surrey and returned to help the *Wrexham Star* with Enoch Moss and the Fletcher brothers, Chris and Alf, who ran a small firm of printers in an old chapel in Abbot Street, Wrexham. I had swapped my square-nosed Morris Cowley for a Fiat 509A PH1824 in Guildford. It was an open two-seater and since the Old Vicarage had no garage, I had to leave it out in the road. George was a furnace-man in the steelworks and kept the Railway Inn opposite the Old Vicarage. He was an old hand with cars and had owned and used Ford Model T's. He was loud in their praise and admired their basic ruggedness. He used to boast that his Ford had never let him down – even when he'd 'run' a big-end on a trip to Rhyl with passengers. 'I was determined to get home. I took the sump off and, made me a new bearing out of the sole of a boot. I'd lost the sump oil so I got some lard from a butcher and filled the sump. I got home safely.'

From the kindness of his heart he arranged a shelter for my Fiat behind his Railway Inn. It's only now I realise how kind he was to me. I must have been, at times, a bit of a nuisance getting my car out at the odd hours a busy pressman kept.

Those are cheerful memories of a good friend, but I must come to the tragedy of Gresford. Saturday, September 22nd, 1934. That morning will always stand out in my memory. It was a cold rainy morning, about 5 o'clock, and I'd just had a very disturbing telephone call from my brother-in-law to be, Les George. His father, a surface worker at Gresford, had phoned home to suggest that Les should get in touch with me: there was something very wrong at the Pit. 'It's full of dust and we can't phone through from the top of the pit to the bottom.' This coincided with another telephone message from my fiancé, Verlie George. She was a Staff Nurse in the Wrexham War Memorial Hospital and she, like everyone else at the Nurses Home, had been woken up in the early hours to prepare for the emergency admission of up to 250 severe accident cases with injuries caused by explosion, burns and crushing. No further explanation had been given but in a mining district none was needed.

As I was getting the Fiat out, George Moulder arrived in his working clothes straight from the Furnaces. He wanted to know why I was up and about so early and I explained I had to get down to Gresford.

'Right, lad, I'll come with you,' he said, and off we went. All the way to the pit I was wondering how I could get on the yard. There would surely be a policeman on the gate. To my surprise as soon as we arrived the gate opened. Georgie Moulder chuckled. 'It's not just good luck,' he said in answer to the question I hadn't asked. 'They think I'm a rescue man come to help.'

After a quick look around, I went to the lamp-room and asked the lampman, 'How many lamps out?' 'Two hundred and sixty four,' he said and my heart missed a beat.

In the cold rainy daylight, I saw a frieze of men and women waiting for news on bank tops overlooking the yard. Lorries were delivering men and tools and – this seemed strange to me – thousands of conical red hand held fire extinguishers. Not much use when a coal mine was on fire, I thought. After some more searching around for stories of what had happened, though of course no official statements were yet being made, I was told some men had got out of the pit from a part not affected by the explosion, had gone home to reassure wives and relatives, returned to Gresford and been ready to go down to Dennis Pit to see if they could help.

I had seen all I wanted to and drove the Fiat down to Abbot Street. Alf Fletcher, who worked the Linotype, had got the 'pot' which holds the hot metal for casting up to working temperature so I sat down and wrote my story. Alf and I set out the single 'forme', locked up the type and Alf got it on the big flat press and the *Star* was out with the story.

I was dismayed to find that the Colliery Office, in reply to a query from Buckingham Palace, had said the 'number of men at risk was a hundred'. Even on the next day the official figures stood at seven dead and 102 trapped underground, but I knew how many lamps were out and that for every lamp there was a man underground.

By three o'clock on that desolate Saturday afternoon I was at the Racecourse ground to report a soccer match. Wrexham were playing Tranmere Rovers and later it became clear that many of the miners had worked a double shift (including the fatal Friday night) so they would be free to watch the game. By the time the match started the *Star* had appeared and I was the subject of a good deal of criticism around the ground since my figures were so much higher than those given in the official announcement.

Already collections were being made for a Gresford fund there: ambulance men held Red Cross blankets (part I thought of the usual football first-aid kit) and held them out for thrown pennies, a novel way to start a fund that grew mightily over the next years. We had decided to sponsor such a fund on behalf of the *Star* and the next day I traced Bert Hampson, the mayor, to his usual fishing ground on the Dee and suggested that a Gresford Fund be started. He agreed with enthusiasm.

Wrexham, on that gloomy September evening, was lifeless and dead, numbed by a tragedy so great that many people were still very reluctant to believe what had happened. I had been so busy during the long day that only now – and with some guilt – remembered that I had promised to pick up Verlie from the Nurses Home at the War Memorial Hospital to take her home to Long Lane. When I found her she was cold and tired. The nursing staff had been working nonstop since 5am, organising the transfer of existing patients and preparing wards and theatres for the arrival of the injured. It was only after she was back home that she had time to notice she'd been working all day with her uniform on top of her nightie.

When we got to Vale View, Long Lane, we found Verlie's father and mother and the family shocked and shaken. Her father Sam George, check weighman at the colliery, had lost his job (one of the 1600 jobs lost in the explosion). John Arthur Harrop, Gresford Colliery Secretary and a fellow member of the Brake Wesleyan Chapel was dying of pneumonia and had been kept in ignorance of the terrible happenings at the pit which was his main purpose in life. The whole tragic tale became clearer as the weekend wore on. The first rescue team down the pit got into difficulties and men were lost at once. Gradually all rescue efforts were abandoned. I spoke to one of the early men down and he told me that looking up one roadway was like looking at a furnace.

The shaft was capped to keep the air out and smother the fires but explosions blew off part of the capping and another man died. It was six months before work could be started again, and men, after months of training and equipped with Siegbe Gorman apparatus, were able to enter the pit.

Tragedies on this scale shape the outlook of the whole community, just as the family and the church and the school shape it too; and this was the community I grew up in. The coalmines have now gone; the steelworks has gone; the railways have gone – but the memories remain and the community remains. It has been said that history is for the community what memory is for the individual and in this sense this account, not of what motivates kings and statesmen but of the experiences that give a small community its attitudes, values and traditions, is an account of the shaping of my values and my life.

This is the 'Old Vicarage' as it was in our day. To the left is the high level water tank supplying the locomotive water column.

Hugh, left, and Geoff Charles and between Dorothy Davies-Jones of Mountain Ash – a cousin, taken in 1916.

S.C. Hughes.

Typical of the Welshman who seemed to occupy every niche of the public life of the Welsh Village of that time was Samuel Charles Hughes, related to the Charles family of Brymbo. He was Parish Clerk, a Wesleyan local Preacher, a member of the Public Hall Committee, an Oddfellow and a Good Templar, and he had charge of the forerunner of modern Labour Exchange. He was the Secretary of the Brymbo District of the 'Queen's Nursing Association', and a widower with a son. His sister, Ellen Esther, was his housekeeper and during the bad days of the general strike and the miners strikes after the 1914/1918 war she played a large part in the setting up o f 'Soup Kitchens' for the children of the strikers.

A cousin of my grandfather Thomas Charles was Tom Price,
born in Maelor View, Brymbo. Tom Price was a prominent
trade unionist who emigrated to Australia and became
the first Labour Prime Minister of South Australia.
He was given a great welcome when he visited Wales in 1908.
This picture is of a visit he made to the Old Vicarage,
and shows left to right front row
Mrs Thomas Charles, Mr Tom Price, Mrs Price, Mr Thomas Charles
and his American grand-daughter. Amongst those in the back row are
the Rev. Richard Jones-Williams who married Jennie, daughter of
Thomas and Mary Charles, Mr Peter Williams, General Manager of
Brymbo Steel Company, Mr and Mrs Aubrey Charles and Mrs Dorothy
Carrington, Prince of Wales Hotel.

When the College of Nursing celebrated its twenty-fifth Anniversary with a Garden Party at Buckingham Palace, two Brymbo Members of the College attended, Nurses J.E. Reade (Mrs John Charles) (centre) and Nurse E. Davies (right).

Brymbo Home Defence Volunteers.
This was the First World War version of the 'Home Guard'.
John Charles is on the left of the picture wearing his usual 'boater'; his
two sons regularly went with him to the firing range and were given
the run of the Army's manuals on the famous Lee Enfield rifles which
they studied with small boys' enthusiasm.

Bethel Chapel, which played a major role in our lives.
The chapel was opened on July 11th 1892 by the Rev. John Evans,
Eglwys-bach, one of the shining lights of the Wesleyan Pulpit.
Connecting train times for the event are printed in the hand bill.

Sunday School Demonstration,

BRYMBO DISTRICT,

To be held on MONDAY, JULY 18th, 1892.

Order of Procession with Tabulated Statement.

No.		No. on Register.	Average Attendance.	No. of Teachers.
1.	English Wesleyans, Brymbo	250	114	16
2.	Welsh Methodist, Brymbo (Engedi)	347	193	32
3.	Welsh Baptist (Tabernacl) including Penrhos Branch	432	265	31
4.	Welsh Independent (Bryn Sion)	180	160	20
5.	English Presbyterians (Black Lane)	80	50	6
6.	Welsh Wesleyans (Bethel)	295	164	20
7.	English Baptists, Lodge	......	......	...
8.	English Free Methodist Lodge	......	......	...
9.	Welsh Methodist (Bethania) Lodge	140	100	17

All the Schools will meet at 2 O'CLOCK P.M.. PROMPT, near the Top Schools,—join in procession, in the order as stated above, and proceed along the following route : —

Through Bryn Sion, Halcog, Green, along Queen's Road, passing Pen-y-garth and the National Schools, along High Street, Foundry Road, Wrexham Road, taking the first turning off Wrexham Road, and proceeding along Top Road, Lodge, down Hill Street, Lodge, returning to Brymbo, along Nant Road, Mount Road, Church Road and High Street, as far as the English Wesleyan Chapel.

The Lodge Schools will leave the procession when near Mr. O. P. Jones's Shop, Lodge.

The Bryn Sion, English Presbyterians and Bethel Schools will leave the procession when near the New Welsh Wesleyan Chapel.

The Tabernacl will leave the procession when near the Cross, the Engedi and English Wesleyans proceeding up High Street to the respective Chapels.

By kind permission of Mr. Nathan Parry, all the Schools will adjourn to Brymbo Hall Park after Tea.

MEREDITH WILLIAMS, Hon. Secretary.

The importance to Brymbo of the Sunday School Movement can be gauged from the Hand-bill headed 'Sunday School Demonstration' of 1892, with its remarkable count of participating scholars, 9 Chapels with 1724 scholars took part.

Brymbo children had to walk to Pentre Broughton to school until Brymbo's Council Schools were built in 1911. Amongst the guests at the opening ceremony were Peter Williams, Edward Roberts 'Bryn Coch', Robert Williams (Builder) and Thomas Charles with his grand-daughter, daughter of T. Owen.Charles, owner and editor of a newspaper in Scranton, U.S.A.

Brymbo West.

Green, Brymbo.

Parish Church, Brymbo.

Brymbo Council School, Standard Six, C.1918.
On floor sitting: George Lloyd, Geoffrey Charles, Dick Holiwell,
Billy Roden, Gwynfryn Wynne, Winston Williams, Hugh Davies, N.K.
First row, seated: Ivor Roberts, Harold Fisher Davies, Ceridwen
Griffiths, - Evans, Martha Davies, Olwen Edwards, - - Roberts, N.K.
First row, standing: N.K., Matilda Williams, N.K., Evelyn Hughes,
Evelyn Thomas, Ceridwen Jones, - - Griffiths, Martha Roberts, N.K.
Second row, standing: N.K., N.K., N.K., John Edward Davies, Maelor
Peters, N.K., N.K., Seth Lloyd.

Brymbo Parish Church.
With the Vicar, the Rev. H.J. Williams is the Bishop of St Asaph and
members of the Parish Church Choir, including Cliff Lloyd,
H. Venables, Archie Venables, Arthur Johnson, G. Rogers,
Norman Roberts, and Ronnie Matthias.

Brymbo Middle Crossing as we knew it.
The 'Old Vicarage' is just out of sight to the left of the picture.

After photographing the G.W.R. tank with its train
on the Mold branch I turned around and saw two G.W.R. tanks
at the water column, so well-known to us when engines 'primed'
and showered us with dirty water.

'Brymbo Middle Box' as it was when I last saw it. On the left of the picture is the line to the Water Column, in the centre of the picture the line to Minera, and the junction of the line to the steel works, and on the extreme right the line to Wrexham.

This is the steep curve at the end of the '1 in 34 bank' which caused so much trouble to the heavy Hook Norton ore trains.

North Western *'pick-up' goods on Prince of Wales Crossing.*

Great Western *Pannier Tank with 'pick-up' goods on Prince of Wales Crossing.*

*This is one of the many photographs taken by John Charles in the
1890's and now in the Clwyd Archives. It shows the L.N.W.R. Mold
Branch near its junction with the G.W.R. Minera Branch, the old
G.W.R. Goods Shed, the old Engine Shed, the old 'Public Hall', and in
the background the Steel Works.*

This John Charles picture is of women and children holding loaves. (Had there been a strike?). They are standing on Railway Road Bridge, and behind them is Bryn Sion Chapel and Clayton Road, and not a council house in sight.

The great depression hit Brymbo district badly.
I happened on pictures of 'Coal pickers' on burning colliery waste tips at Southsea. Here I found pickers looking for what coal they could find to warm their homes, waiting for the 'spoil waggons' to be unloaded.

An old bicycle has a freshly picked sack of coal on the frame above the pedals while the two men with the donkey cart are using a different form of transport. Both pictures tell the story of the suffering of those bad days of the 'Hungry Thirties'.

This is a view of the Brymbo Steel Works and Blast Furnaces about 1890. The house overlooked the Great Central Railway's Brymbo Station.

A John Charles picture of the 1890's.
John Charles liked the way the old Beam Engine seen in this picture
of 'Pwll Cadi' had been adapted as a winding engine in the pit.
In the distance is the other Brymbo Station featured in the
'Saturday Night Train Race'.

Another view of the derelict Pwll Cadi Colliery. A footpath from 'Top School' to 'The Lodge' passed close to these remains.

Cymau.
Brymbo Steel Works chimneys on the skyline emphasize
the rural nature of this industrial area.

Pool Top, Brymbo.

Steelworkers.
Four generations of ironworkers produced these four men, making
steel by the Basic Open Hearth method. This later gave way to the
Electric Arc Furnaces.
A by-product of the open Hearth process was 'Basic Slag'. The slag
was poured into a ladle, a piece of steel inserted and the ladle and its
contents left to cool. Then a strange locomotive, called 'Basic' which
we have mentioned used its crane to pull out several similar masses
of hardened slag, placed them on flat waggons which it propelled to a
small factory with the inelegant name of 'Muck Works'.
Here the slag was ground, bagged, and loaded on waggons
for use as an agricultural fertiliser.

Steelworks Trip to Southport c.1925.
on mudguard: R. Matthias, Driver - Stapley, Jack Simonds,
H.G. Charles, F. Harris, Mr D. Lawson, R.V. Williams, V. Venables,
N.K., N.K., N.K., I. Matthias, P. Jones, -- Hallam, N.K., P. Griffiths,
- Williams, G.M. Jones, H.S. Rogers, N.K., N.K., N.K., N.K., N.K.,
Clown Ted Lettsome.

*The morning after the Luftwaffe's visit. The Road smashed up,
closed by rubble, the small shop blown off its foundations
and the Cinema showing signs of damage.*

*Sightseers watch a repair gang working on the damage to the Queens
Head caused by the detonation of the unexploded bomb.*

The wooden shuttering shows where the Bomb disposal men
had to dig their way down to the unexploded bomb,
ten days' work revealed the bomb too dangerous to be safely defused.
Mr Harry Grainger's house and shop were severely damaged,
and later demolished.

The morning after the Luftwaffe's visit.
Verlie and I inspect the damage to the Cinema.
In view of the war-time slogan, 'Careless talk costs lives'.
The film on show that night 'Tell no tales' seems appropriate.
The cinema was later demolished and a garage opened on the site.

Brymbo, once an Iron Coal and steel village turned its back on the Industrial Revolution, and is now building houses for the shopkeepers of Wrexham. These houses here are built on the former LNWR line from Mold to Brymbo.

The site of the 'Prince of Wales Crossing', Brymbo

A more recent picture shows the Crossing Cottage and the Prince of Wales Hotel and a wilderness of shrubbery where the Railway was.